Found
and Practice
of Healing Touch

Authored by:

Joel G. Anderson PhD, CHTP
Lisa C. Anselme RN, BLS, HN-BC, CHTP/I
Laura K. Hart PhD, MEd, RN, CHTP/I

Healing Beyond Borders
Lakewood, CO

Foundations and Practice of Healing Touch

Copyright © 2017 by Healing Touch International, Inc.

ALL RIGHTS RESERVED. No part of this book may be used, reproduced, stored in a retrieval system, or transmitted, in any form or by any means-electronic, internet usage, mechanical, photocopy, recording, or otherwise - without prior written permission of the publisher, except for brief quotations embodied in critical articles and reviews.

Authors
Joel G. Anderson PhD, CHTP
Lisa C. Anselme RN, BLS, HN-BC, CHTP/I
Laura K. Hart PhD, MEd, RN, CHTP/I

Cover Design: Cat Miller
Cover Photo: Joel Anderson
Illustrations: Lisa Anselme
Figures & Algorithms: Joel Anderson
Technique Photography: Cat Miller

A Publication of Healing Beyond Borders
445 Union Boulevard, Suite 105
Lakewood, CO 80228
USA
www.HealingBeyondBorders.org
303.989.7982

ISBN: 978-0-692-87756-2

The authors and publisher have exerted every effort to ensure and confirm the accuracy of the information presented and to describe generally accepted practices. However, the authors and publisher are not responsible for errors or omissions or for any consequences from application of the information in this book and make no warranty, express or implied, with respect to the practice, procedures or content of the publication. The authors and publisher shall not be liable for any special, consequential, or exemplary damages resulting, in whole or part, from the readers' use of, or reliance upon, the material contained herein.

Foreword

The authors wish to acknowledge the wisdom of historical and contemporary healers, practitioners, scientists, and educators who have supported the bringing together of the Healing Touch Certificate Program over several decades. The present text serves as an extension of this grounded foundation in healing and would not have been possible without this previous work. Our intention in writing and compiling this text has been not only to bring together all of this wisdom into one place, but also to move forward the practice and education of Healing Touch. Original source material for all techniques, foundation work, and the philosophy of healing have been researched and referenced, along with more recent theoretical understandings and scientific findings. New content has been envisioned through guidance and grounded in the foundations of energy work, with the intent of raising the vibration of the certificate program in congruence with the state of the science and practice of Healing Touch. Our hope is that this text will serve as a thorough introduction to the foundations and practice of Healing Touch to students and novices, as well as a reference and starting point for additional study for practitioners and instructors. The authors gratefully acknowledge those authors and instructors who have supported and nurtured the education in and practice of Healing Touch over these many years.

Healing Beyond Borders
Educating and Certifying the Healing Touch®

Contents

CHAPTER	Foundations and Practice of Healing Touch	
1	**Introduction to Healing Touch**	**9**
	Healing Touch and Biofield Therapies	9
	Philosophies of Healing	11
	Healing Beyond Borders Vision and Mission	12
	Core Values	12
2	**Preparation and Evolution of the Healer**	**17**
	Basic Tenets of the Practitioner in Service	17
	Attributes of the Heart	18
	Transformational Development	19
	Self Care and Well-Being	19
	Healing Presence and Environment	21
	Principles of Holistic Health	22
3	**Holistic and Energetic Foundations of Healing**	**27**
	Foundations of Holism and Energetic Patterns	27
	The Human Energy System	27
	The Biofield	28
	The Chakras	32
	The Meridians	32
	The Nadis	32
	The Four Energy Bodies	36
4	**Framework for the Healing Touch Session**	**39**
	Introduction to the Framework for a Healing Touch Session	39
	Assessment and Documentation	41
	Language for Describing Energetic Findings	48
	Advanced Healing Touch Session	49
	Advanced Healer Preparation	49
	Hara Alignment	51
	Core Star Expansion	52
	Spinning Chakras	53
	Etheric Vitality	54

CHAPTER

5   Healing Touch Techniques   55

Introduction to Healing Touch and Biofield Therapy Techniques	55
Celestial and Ketheric Repatterning	56
Chakra Connection	58
Chakra Energizing	58
Chakra Spread	60
Chelation	62
Deep Auric Clearing	64
Etheric Template Repatterning	66
Field Repatterning	67
Fifth Layer Healing	69
Glymphatic System Support	70
Hopi Technique	72
Laser	74
Lymphatic Clearing	76
Modified Mesmeric Clearing	80
Noel's Mind Clearing	82
Scudder Meridian Clearing	84
Siphon	87
Spinal Clearing and Energizing	88
Spinal Flush	89
Spiral Meditation	92

6   Energetic Patterns and Clinical Application of Healing Touch   95

Applications of Laser, Field Repatterning, Chakra Connection
    Pain Ridge, Pain Spike, Suture, Wound Closure
    Headache Management
	95

Evidence-Based Practice of Healing Touch	100
Integrative Health Care	101

7   Professional Practice and Ethics   103

Healing Touch Code of Ethics / Standards of Practice	103
Ethical Practice and Professional Ethics	105
Legal Aspects of Biofield Therapy Practice	108
Practicum and Certification	109
Case Management	111

Appendix

HTI Healing Touch Certificate Program	113
Course Descriptions	113
Notice of Privacy Practices	115
Health Care Policy and Procedure	118
Sample Consent	120
Assessment & Documentation Sample Form	121
Follow-up Documentation Sample Form	123

Chapter 1

INTRODUCTION TO HEALING TOUCH

Healing Touch and Biofield Therapies

"In every culture and in every medical tradition before ours, healing was accomplished by moving energy." Albert Szent-Györgi (1960)

The idea that all life is sustained by a universal life energy has existed throughout human history and continues. Theories of quantum physics state that reality as we know it is made up entirely of energy in its many forms, with energy fields vibrating at different frequencies (Oschman, 2003). These alterations in frequency allow some energies to be made visible and tangible as matter and others as invisible but known, such as gravity and the electromagnetic spectrum. The idea and paradigm of a human energy field or biofield flows through philosophy, from ancient times to the present (Bradley,1987; Brekke & Schultz, 2006; Erickson, 2007; Oschman, 2000; Todaro-Franceschi, 2008). Throughout history, humanity has taken the view of an integrated world in which communication happens between humans and their surroundings, with a life force permeating and connecting the human with the environment. Balance or imbalance in this energy exchange was the harbinger of disease or illness, as well as the source of health and well-being (Bradley, 1987; Graham, 1990; Krieger, 1979). This energy has been described in a similar fashion with like characteristics and function across cultures and throughout time, bringing with it vitality, healing, awakening, and transformation.

Hands on healing and energy therapies and traditions have been used by all cultures for millennia. Ancient civilizations, including those of Egypt, Babylonia, Assyria, Phoenicia, India, Iran, Greece, and Rome, developed schools of healing that drew upon wisdom traditions to train and initiate healers (Jain & Mills, 2009; Leder & Krucoff, 2008; Levin, 2009; Wang & Hermann, 2006). Evidence of energy healing can be found in the *Huang Ti Ching Su Wen*, known as *The Esoteric Scripture of the Yellow Emperor*, from the Chinese Han dynasty (206 B.C.–220 A.D.) and the foundation for Traditional Chinese Medicine (Wang & Hermann, 2006). Energy medicine is depicted in the hieroglyphs of the Egyptian 3rd dynasty and the time of the stepped pyramid at Saqqara. Hippocrates, the Father of Western Medicine, acknowledged the existence of the human biofield or energy as flowing from the hands. The chakras and energy system of the Indian culture and the Eastern balancing of yin and yang reflect these ancient energetic principles.

In addition to these ancient traditions, the use of energy from sources outside of the body has been recognized for healing properties for centuries. Bloodstone or red iron ore was mined in Africa over 100,000 years ago for healing and ceremonial purposes (Oschman, 2000). Lodestone, a naturally magnetized piece of the mineral magnetite, was used for healing by the ancient Egyptians, Chinese, and Greeks. Franz Mesmer began using magnets for healing in the late 18th century, with patients feeling "unusual current" in their bodies through the use of magnets. Mesmer later discovered he could produce the same sensations using only his hands. Even electric eels have been used in ancient times for the treatment of the sick (Oschman, 2000).

Monastic and Medieval orders of healers continued the ancient hands on healing philosophies through the practice of healing traditions from insight received during meditation (Levin, 2009). A central concept for all of these energetic, healing traditions was the use of perception of the human energy field and the use of touch and intention to affect change in the subtle energies of the human body. These subtle energies were seen as supporting existence of life itself, and having effects on the body, mind, and spirit (Jain & Mills, 2009). Additionally, these traditions recognized healing as a serious profession, with requisite training, preparation, and grounding in specific techniques with mentorship and guidance from theory and practice (Jain & Mills, 2009; Levin, 2009). A contemporary approach to these ancient energy healing therapies that acknowledges the training and preparation of the healer is Healing Touch.

Healing Touch is a relaxing, nurturing, **heart-centered, biofield (energy) therapy**. Gentle, intentional touch assists in balancing physical, mental, emotional and spiritual well-being. Healing Touch assists in creating a coherent and balanced energy field, **supporting one's inherent ability to heal**. It is safe for all ages and works in harmony with and may be integrated with standard medical care.

Healing Touch is classified by the National Institutes of Health as a biofield therapy and nursing intervention that contains a group of standardized, noninvasive **techniques that clear, energize, and balance the human and environmental energy fields**. Healing Touch may be used to address the North American Nursing Diagnosis Association (NANDA-1) diagnosis of "Imbalanced Energy Field". Healing Touch is used in collaboration with other Western medicine and integrative approaches to health and healing. Healing Touch is used in a wide variety of environments including hospitals, long-term care facilities, private practices, hospices, and spas and is taught in universities, medical and nursing schools, and other settings internationally. Healing Touch provides a sense of calm, wholeness, and healing.

Philosophies of Healing

The words 'health' and 'healing' share the same root word 'haelen', which means "to make whole" (Leder & Krucoff, 2008). Healing enables a person who is sick to re-integrate and recover the equilibrium between the mind, body, spirit, and environment, moving toward wholeness even in the presence of ongoing challenges. Healing is multidimensional and beyond curing. This process is often aided by touch, which has become synonymous with healing itself. For example, one might be known as having "the healing touch". Touch serves as a way to support the connection between the self and others, disrupting pain, improving incapacities, and reframing illness. Touch is fundamental to the practice of nursing and, thus, healing (Wardell & Engebretson, 2001). Touch is so key that it is recognized as an intervention in the Nursing Interventions Classification Code (Wardell & Engebretson, 2001).

A natural and self-directed process, healing is innate (King, 2005) and has been recognized in nursing care since Florence Nightingale first wrote about it in *Notes on Nursing* in 1859. As with nursing, the practice of Healing Touch and promotion of healing focuses on meeting the physical, social, spiritual, and emotional needs of an individual through empathy (Şenyuva, Kaya, Işik, & Bodur, 2014). The self-compassion, or ability to be compassionate to oneself, that is developed by the practitioner of Healing Touch allows for compassionate action toward the patient. This compassionate care allows the practitioner as healer to address the suffering of illness, whether it be physical, emotional, mental, or spiritual, with tenderness by recognizing the dimensions of kindness, mindfulness, and common humanity (Şenyuva et al., 2014). This sense of compassion for self and others is foundational to philosophies of healing and essential to the practice of Healing Touch.

The concept of energy exchange on some level between individuals is the foundation of healing techniques and biofield therapies such as Healing Touch (Oschman, 2002). References to these energetic interactions are found not only in ancient, wisdom texts, but also in the psychotherapeutic literature of Freud, who proposed that the balancing of energy between the practitioner and patient unconsciously affects the physical, emotional, and mental health of the patient. This exchange of energy is facilitated by communication between the electromagnetic and subtle energies of the practitioner and patient through entrainment.

Entrainment is the synchronization of two energy fields or rhythms. Think about the clocks in a clock shop. The pendulums of the clocks all swing in the same rhythm and in sync because the clocks have entrained. Placing a new clock into the shop, you would find that it would entrain with all of the other clocks. A similar phenomenon occurs during energy healing, facilitating the exchange of energy, intention, and compassion from a place of heart-centered healing. This is supported by science. As the heart generates the largest biomagnetic field of any organ in the body, and given that cellular regulation can be influenced by pulsing electromagnetic fields, the energy field of the heart is most likely involved in effects of Healing Touch. In fact, the frequencies used in conventional clinical electrotherapies are within the frequency spectrum of the magnetic field of the heart. This concept of entrainment will be described in more detail in a later chapter. For now, it is important to acknowledge the vital role of compassion and empathy in the healing process and as a part of the practice of Healing Touch.

In a holistic model of care, the **primary role of the practitioner** is to provide a healing connection that allows a patient to reconnect with the self. The focus is on understanding patterns of connection and disconnection. When achieved within, a state of equilibrated mental perspective of mindfulness exists and is therefore available to be experienced by others through entrainment and intention. Intention is a mental state directed toward achieving a goal that is a crucial component of the healing process. Mariano describes intention as "the conscious awareness of being in the present moment, a volitional act of love, and a conscious alignment of essence and purpose allowing the highest good to flow through a healing intervention (Mariano, 2016)." These aspects of the healing philosophy will be discussed in greater detail in later chapters.

Feinstein and Eden (2008) have distilled the concepts of energy medicine and biofield therapies into what they call the six pillars of energy medicine. These pillars will be described in further detail throughout this text. As an introduction these pillars include: the **scope** or reach of energy medicine; the **efficiency** of the therapy; its **practicality**; the support and **empowerment** of **patients** through biofield therapies; the **alignment** of these therapies with **quantum** physics; and the **holistic orientation** of therapies and philosophy.

Healing Beyond Borders Vision and Mission

Healing Touch International, Inc., now doing business as Healing Beyond Borders, is the Healing Touch non-profit professional organization founded by Janet Mentgen RN, in 1996. Healing Beyond Borders is dedicated to spreading healing, light, and love worldwide, and supporting the heart-centered practice and teaching of Healing Touch, Continuing Education, Research, Health Care Integration, and Professional Development. Support services are provided for the general public, Students, Practitioners, Instructors, and those interested in healing.

Core Values

Healing Touch International identified Seven Core Vales in 2003. These core values of Healing Touch are foundational to the spiritual dimension of this work and guide Healing Touch Practitioners in life. These Core Values support and underpin the practice and teaching of Healing Touch.

1. Integrity

According to Trout (1990),

> A person with integrity has a strong sense of self, sets and maintains healthy boundaries, is forthright and natural, profound and candid, impartial and reliable. To be impeccable, our integrity must consistently pervade our thoughts and actions...Others can feel safe with this level of integrity, allowing healing to occur at the highest level (pp. 95, 106).

Additionally, the integrity of the field of the practitioner is an essential aspect of overall integrity. Writes Bennett, "...gradations of wholeness... are determined by the extent or degree to which a given object is itself and does not merge into something that is not itself (Bennett, 1956, p. 6)."

2. Unconditional Love

Unconditional love is a way of being. Unconditional love is impersonal and detached in nature, transcending personal love. Unconditional love supports progression into a spiritual dimension of healing.

3. Heart-Centered

When heart-centered, one leaves personal issues behind and enters a Universal state of consciousness, opening the heart chakra. When you are centered in your heart you open to oneness with all. The heart chakra is the locus where the act of centering is sustained, so that all aspects of the work are expressed through the heart chakra via the human attributes of love and compassion (Kunz, 2004a). The practitioner centers through directing his/her awareness inward and operating from heart-centered decisions as evidenced by the presence of caring and compassion (Freel & Hart, 1999).

4. Respect

Respect is the act of giving attention, consideration, and/or esteem. Healing Touch Practitioners respect others' beliefs and practices, honoring their autonomy, growth and self-empowerment. Patients are respected and valued regardless of sex, race, creed, age, gender identity, sexual orientation, or health condition.

5. Self Care

The goals of self care are to enhance our physical, emotional, mental and spiritual well-being through continued learning, self growth, and evolution. It is only through cultivating our own health, self growth and well-being that we are able to support and accompany others along their healing path.

6. Community

Community refers to a collection of people who interact with one another and whose common interests or characteristics form the basis for a sense of unity or belonging (Spradley, 1996).

Community in Healing Touch is the interconnectedness we experience with each other, and the collective strength that flows from sacred community. Community involves acting in a beneficent way (Page, 2003). Community is about interconnectedness, cooperation, honor, and respect for each other.

7. Service

According to Remen (1996),

> Service rests on the basic premise that the nature of life is sacred, that life is a holy mystery which has an unknown purpose. Everyone who has ever served through the history of time serves the same thing. We are servers of the wholeness and mystery of life.

Service occurs in a relationship between equals, which strengthens and renews itself, sustaining both. Service is an act of helpful activity. The three major factors that affect the quality and effectiveness of our service to others include creating a safe space, honoring the process and staying on purpose (Trout, 1990).

References

Bennett, J. G. (1956). *The foundations of a natural philosophy.* London: Hodder and Stroughton.

Bradley, D. (1987). Energy fields: Implications for nurses. *Journal of Holistic Nursing,* 5, 257-263.

Brekke, M., & Schultz, E. (2006). Energy theories: Modeling and role-modeling. In H. Erickson (Ed.), *Modeling and role-modeling: A view from the client's world* (pp. 33-67). Cedar Park, TX: Unicorns Unlimited.

Erickson, H. (2007). Philosophy and theory of holism. *Nursing Clinics of North America,* 42, 139-163.

Feinstein, D., & Eden, D. (2008). Six pillars of energy medicine: Clinical strengths of a complementary paradigm. *Alternative Therapies in Health and Medicine,* 14, 44–54.

Freel, M.I., & Hart, L.K. (1999). Holistic Nursing In *Nurses's Handbook of alternative and complementary therapies.* Springhouse, PA: Springhouse Corporation, 61-82.

Graham, H. (1990). *Time, energy, and the psychology of healing.* Philadelphia, PA: Jessica Kingsley.

Jain, S., & Mills, P. J. (2010). Biofield therapies: Helpful or full of hype? A best evidence synthesis. *International Journal of Behavioral Medicine,* 17(1), 1-16.

King, R. P.(2005). The integration of Healing Touch with conventional care at the Scripps Center for Integrative Medicine. *Explore: The Journal of Science and Healing*, 1, 144–145.

Krieger, D. (1979). *The Therapeutic Touch: How to use your hands to help or to heal.* Englewood Cliffs, NJ: Prentice-Hall.

Kunz, D. (2004a). Beneficial influences on the chakras. In D. Kunz & D Kreiger (Eds.) *The spiritual dimensions of therapeutic touch.* (pp. 149-155). Rochester, VT: Bear & Co.

Kunz, D.(2004b). Chakras and the therapeutic touch process: Introductory comments. In D. Kunz & D Kreiger (Eds.)*The spiritual dimensions of therapeutic touch.* (pp. 132-133). Rochester, VT: Bear & Co.

Leder, D., & Krucoff, M. W, (2008). The touch that heals: The uses and meanings of touch in the clinical encounter. *Journal of Alternative and Complementary Medicine*, 14, 321–328.

Levin, J. (2009). How faith heals: A theoretical model. *Explore: The Journal of Science and Healing*, 5, 77–96.

Mariano, C. (2016) Holistic Nursing: Scope and Standards of Practice in Dossey, B., Keegan, L., Barrere, C., Blaszko Helming, M., Shields, D., Avino, K. (2016).*Holistic Nursing: A Handbook for Practice* (7th Ed.) Burlington, MA: Jones & Bartlett Learning, p. 53-76.

Oschman, J. L. (2003). *Energy medicine in therapeutics and human performance.* Oxford, England: Butterworth Heinemann.

Oschman, J. (2002). Clinical aspects of biological fields: An introduction for health care professionals. *Journal of Bodywork and Movement Therapies*, 6, 117-125.

Oschman, J. (2000). *Energy medicine: The scientific basis.* New York, NY: Churchill Livingstone.

Page, C., (2003) *Spiritual Alchemy.* Essex, UK: C.W. Daniel Company.

Remen, R.N. (1996).In the Service of Life. *Noetic Sciences Review*. Petaluma, CA: Institute of Noetic Sciences.

Şenyuva, E., Kaya, H., Işik, B., & Bodur, G. (2014). Relationship between self-compassion and emotional intelligence in nursing students. *International Journal of Nursing Practice* 20, 588-596.

Spradley, B. W. (1996). *Community health nursing, concepts and practice,* Fourth Edition, NY: Lippincott.

Todaro-Franceschi, V. (2008). Clarifying the enigma of energy, philosophically speaking. *Nursing Science Quarterly*, 21, 285-290.

Trout, S. (1990). *To see differently: Personal growth and being of service through attitudinal healing.* Alexandria, VA: Three Roses Press.

Wang, K. L., & Hermann, C. (2006). Pilot study to test the effectiveness of healing touch on agitation in people with dementia. *Geriatric Nursing, 27*, 34-40.

Wardell, D. W., & Engebretson, J.(2001). Biological correlates of Reiki touch healing. *Journal of Advanced Nursing*, 33, 439–445.

Chapter 2

PREPARATION AND EVOLUTION OF THE HEALER

Basic Tenets of the Practitioner in Service

A healer always acts in a beneficent manner (Hines, Wardell, Engebretson, Zahourek, & Smith, 2015). The philosophy of Healing Touch is one of extending care to a patient as an act of compassion and service. Practitioners engage in these healing relationships with patients in an effort to alleviate suffering, decrease distress, and provide comfort. These actions highlight the essential humanity of caring and compassion, and Healing Touch provides an avenue by which individuals may serve humanity through compassionate care in a heart-centered fashion. Practitioners of Healing Touch seek and learn about ways of caring for others and promoting self-healing. This compassionate service leads to a shift in awareness on the part of the practitioner (Zahourek, 2012) to one that is heart-centered. This allows for the formation of caring-healing relationships that promote connectedness and wholeness (Jackson, Firtko, and Edenborough, 2007; Swengros et al., 2014).

Healing Touch is not simply an application of a treatment or intervention, but an act of compassionate service with a shared meaning. Holistic nurses and healers speak about this shared meaning as connection on a deeper level with patients that goes beyond simple encounters. What characterizes this connection is fostering a mind-body-spirit connection for the patient that goes beyond a particular ailment or event. Energy healing such as Healing Touch provides a means by which practitioners may use compassion, heart-centered intention and care, as supported by nursing theory, in service to the greater good of humanity, improving the lives of patients and the environment. To do so, practitioners must acknowledge their own levels of wisdom as well as seek preparation and evolution as a healer. This requires knowledge and manifestation of the Attributes of the Heart, transformational development, self care and well-being, and fostering a healing presence and healing environment.

Attributes of the Heart

"There is no greater gift one can offer than the energy of unconditional love." (Brugh Joy, *Joy's Way*)

Dr. Brugh Joy presented a workshop in Denver, Colorado, in 2007 during which he described the five Attributes of the Heart. These are described as follows, as well Joy's method for meditating on these attributes.

The first attribute of the heart is **Unconditional Love**. According to Joy, Unconditional Love

> ...exists before temporality and before eternity. Its influx unites all things together and transforms power into love. It will cause you to fall in love with all of life. It will give you the eye of the heart center that sees things in their richness clearly.

In opening to the first attribute of the heart center, we open to those around us.

The second attribute of the heart center is **Healing Presence**. Discussed in greater detail later in this chapter, Healing Presence "heals, harmonizes, and heightens that which realigns us back into our original intention... [which is] the body's ability to restore and renew itself."

Bringing us to the third attribute of the heart center, **Innate Harmony**, Joy describes Innate Harmony as "that which makes the heart lighter than the feather."

The fourth attribute of the heart center is **Compassion**. Compassion "is the ability to know another directly..." Compassion is being open to and moved by the suffering of others within a perspective of desire to ease their suffering, offering patience, kindness, and non-judgmental understanding, and is inclusive of an awareness of human imperfection including within oneself. Compassion requires empathy and seeks to achieve good in the context of suffering. Empathy is the ability to recognize "the other" as similar to self and makes possible the common experience of action or emotion, embodied simulation versus simple cognitive recognition, and listening without preconception.

Opening to these first four attributes, the fifth attribute of the heart center of **Selfless Service** is achieved.

According to Joy,

> Meditation is fundamental to coming into more expanded states of consciousness. Without it, you tend to have more of the conditioned awareness...the one that is thinking all the time. It's a practice and hopefully it will be an experiential expansion at the feeling level rather than at the thinking level. The Heart Center is a gate into the transpersonal...So the ritual of opening...the heart center is a way of moving away from the temporal,... [and more toward the] eternal.

Joy recommends "practicing 5 minutes per day of pure heart-centered meditation...The degree to which you can make that change is the degree to which you have access to the resources [of the heart]." To do so, pick one of the attributes of the heart center upon which to meditate. Make yourself comfortable.

> When you place your hand caringly, nurturingly, reverently, inspirationally at the heart center, the body fully responds at the heart level. So, light touch onto the heart center announces to the body the fullness of your desire to open to [the attributes of the heart].

Transformational Development

"When I let go of what I am, I become what I might be." Lao Tsu

Healing may take several forms and may be experienced as increased empathy and a feeling of transcendence (Cooperstein, 1992). Healing practitioners often report feeling a sense of self-transcendence and transformation that increases levels of empathy (Hines, Wardell, Engebretson, Zahourek, & Smith, 2015). This occurs most readily through the enhancement of self-compassion for the practitioner (Raab, 2014). Self-compassion is defined as having a sense of mindfulness and awareness, a kindness toward one's self, and a recognition of the common humanity one shares with others (Neff, 2003). Self-compassion is essential for effectiveness in providing patients with empathy, compassion, and understanding (Heffernan, Quinn Griffin, McNulty, & Fitzpatrick, 2010; Şenyuva, Kaya, Işik, & Bodur, 2014). Training in mind-body therapies such as Healing Touch can increase self-compassion through enhancing mindfulness and awareness. Training in Healing Touch provides an opportunity to develop self-compassion, supporting empowerment and transformational development. Education in and practice of Healing Touch fosters positive changes for the self by virtue of its holistic approach and reflective, mindful process. Additionally, a study of nurses and non-nurses involved in Healing Touch training found significant differences between the levels of training in Healing Touch classes, with individuals completing upper level Healing Touch classes having higher scores in spiritual and religious attitudes (Wardell, 2001). These findings suggest that involvement in an energy-based therapy is one way to develop spiritual awareness.

Self Care and Well-Being

Well-being is dependent upon self care. Self care is defined as intentional activities used to restore balance in our lives. The intention, or state of mind, behind self care is oriented toward improving and nourishing self-awareness, self-regulation, and self-efficacy. A lack of self care may lead to a feeling of depletion, which causes burnout, compassion fatigue, stress, and dysfunction.

Suggested activities for self care include the following:

Light exercise and physical activity at least three days per week improves mood as well as productivity.

Reading and journaling increase creativity and activate specific areas of the brain related to positive mood.

Laughter is known to strengthen the immune system, boost energy, and decrease pain. Adults typically laugh infrequently throughout the day, while children laugh hundreds of times on average.

Eating well and drinking plenty of water is essential to well-being and self care. Diets rich in omega-3 fatty acids improve cognitive function and mood. Complex carbohydrates are involved in the release of endorphins, while proteins provide the building blocks needed to keep our bodies functioning properly. Dietary patterns focusing on whole foods, plenty of fruits and vegetables, and whole grains have been shown to promote health and well-being. Hydration is critical for clarity of thought and physical wellness. While the common rule of thumb is considered to be six to eight glasses of water per day, a better rule of thumb is to drink half your weight in ounces of water. For example, a person who weighs 150 pounds, or 68 kilograms, should consume 75 ounces (2.2 liters) of water per day.

Meditation is supported by decades of research indicating its usefulness in decreasing anxiety and stress, as well as improving physiological health and cognitive function.

Spend **time in nature.** The natural environment is restorative and aids in maintaining healthy levels of the stress hormone cortisol.

Taking **time off** is not merely a luxury given that it supports better sleep quality, decreased stress, and improved mood.

Sleep restores cognitive function, improves moods, decreases stress and anxiety, and is vital for restoration of the body, mind, and spirit. Sleep is imperative for the proper function of the Glymphatic System in the brain. Recommendations are for seven to nine hours each night.

Self care supports resilience, which is a protective factor against burnout/compassion fatigue, and is associated with increased mindfulness and self-compassion, as well as improved physical and mental health (Kemper, Mo, & Khayyam, 2015; Olson & Kemper, 2014). Training in mind-body therapies improves resilience (Fortney, Luchterhand, Zakletskaia, Zgierska, & Rake, 2013) through "mentoring relationships, achieving life balances and spirituality, positive emotions and personal growth and reflections [as] protective factors" (Jackson, Firtko, and Edenborough, 2007; p. 7). Positive emotion improves cognitive function, social support, mental health, and overall well-being.

Chapter 2

Healing Presence and Environment

Nurses often recognize the impact of entering and leaving the field of a patient, which is part of the effect of healing presence (Bossi et al., 2008). The term 'healing presence' is defined as a complex characteristic of a healer that promotes a beneficial, therapeutic, and/or positive spiritual experience in the patient (McDonough-Means, Kreitzer, & Bell, 2004). The term has its origins in religion and philosophy. Within these contexts, it is a psychological or spiritual perception of invisible "essence." Presence may not only facilitate self-healing in the patient, but also within the practitioner. It has been described as an interpersonal, intrapersonal, and transpersonal phenomenon.

Holistic healing occurs when the practitioner is fully present. When a practitioner is fully present with a patient, this increases levels of trust and safety. Presence is a way of using oneself as an instrument of healing (Slater, 1999). Given that presence involves mutual exchange, practitioners and patients both benefit.

Healing involves caring connections and relationships. Healers facilitate these connections through presence, intentionality, and use of various modalities and approaches (Kenny, 2012). A full sense of awareness and appreciation creates caring-healing relationships based on connectedness and wholeness (Cowling, 2002; Smith, Zahourek, Hines, Engebretson, & Wardell, 2013). A sense of being supported, of having an advocate, is an outcome resulting from healing presence.

Two dimensions of presence are often recognized: the physical or "being there," and the psychological or "being with." Physical presence involves body-to-body proximity and the requisite skills of seeing, examining, touching, doing, and hearing. Psychological presence requires a practitioner to have skills of listening, attending to, caring, empathy, being nonjudgmental, and accepting. Full presence is "being there" in the context of another, and includes psychological as well as physical presence and is the embodiment of empathy, caring, and use of self in a face-to-face interaction.

These dimensions can be taken further into the realm of healing through therapeutic presence and transcendent presence. Therapeutic presence entails a spirit-to-spirit connection and requires that a practitioner have skills of centering and grounding, intentionality, intuitive knowing, imagery, and connecting. Transcendent presence is an exchange of energy between the practitioner and patient that is transforming and spiritual in quality and moves beyond interactional to transpersonal. It is felt as peaceful, comforting, and harmonious, and goes beyond the therapeutic use of self. It is achieved when oneness is felt between the practitioner and patient.

A critical part of a healer's journey is recognition of how to create an environment in which healing can occur. Healing Touch practitioners exhibit therapeutic presence through the creation of an accepting,

Principles of Holistic Health
Human beings are energy fields.
There is a unity and interdependence within the mind, body, and spirit.
Health involves a sense of unity (connectedness or oneness) with the self and the cosmos.
Health is a process that may include disease.
Health is the dynamic evolution (continuous process of emergence) toward balanced integration.
Healing, when viewed holistically, is not predictable in terms of time frame, cause, or outcome.
Energy fields are constantly interacting.
The Source is experienced or known through joy, beauty, love, light, peace, power, and life.
Changes in health can occur through experiential learning. Experiential learning is defined as a change in behavior, which occurs as a result of living through an activity, event, or situation.
Spiritual health is necessary for physical, mental, and emotional well-being.

Estby, S.N., Freel, M.I., Hart, L.K., Reese, J.L., Clow, T.J. (1994). A delphi study of the basic principles and corresponding care goals of holistic nursing practice, Journal of Holistic Nursing, Vol. 12 No. 4, December, 402-413.

Used with permission.

Principles of Holistic Health

The human spirit is the core of the person.
Energy fields can become unbalanced as a response to stress in any one of the three domains of body, mind, and spirit.
Healing involves a transformational (second order) change that encompasses the whole person; it requires the involvement of the spiritual, emotional, and intellectual domains, as well as the physical body.
Wellness encompasses increasing openness (acceptance of diversity) and increasing harmony (coherent, high frequency energy fields).
The patient-practitioner relationship is one of equal partnership with different responsibilities.
One's health and disease are manifested in one's lifestyle, habits, and conscious awareness, as well as the body's physical being and energy.
Each health system should be respected for the sources and the tools that it offers, while being challenged to prove its credibility.

Estby, S.N., Freel, M.I., Hart, L.K., Reese, J.L., Clow, T.J. (1994). A delphi study of the basic principles and corresponding care goals of holistic nursing practice, Journal of Holistic Nursing, Vol. 12 No. 4, December, 402-413.

Used with permission.

heart-centered environment in which patients are able to access self-healing abilities (McKivergin, 2000). This establishes a sense of calm for oneself, which fosters a similar environment of calm in one's practice. Healing environments that are calm, soft, and inviting decrease levels of perceived stress for patients (Hines, Wardell, Engebretson, Zahourek, & Smith, 2015).

In a 1994 Delphi survey 17 expert holistic nurse practitioners identified 17 principles of holistic health. These practitioners, who used a wide range of healing modalities in their holistic practice, viewed health as a dynamic process related to open, harmonious, interactive energy fields, and supported a practice model based on holographic perspectives. The principles which they identified, as shown in the figures on pages 22-23, relate to unity, interdependence, evolution, and energy with a strong emphasis on the client's spiritual dimension and a respect and mutuality regarding achievement of goals determined by the client (Estby, Freel, Hart, Reese & Clow, 1994).

Freel and Hart note, "All interventions delivered by all health care systems and their practitioners, regardless of their own individual world views, are holistic in impact. All interventions affect some part of the human system and, therefore, affect the whole system" (Freel & Hart, 1998).

References

Bossi, L. M., Ott, M. J., & DeCristofaro, S. (2008). Reiki as a clinical intervention in oncology nursing practice. Clinical Journal of Oncology Nursing, 12(3), 489-494.

Cooperstein, M. A. (1992). The myths of healing: A summary of research into transpersonal healing experience. Journal of the American Society for Psychical Research, 86, 99-133.

Cowling, R. (2002). Healing as appreciating wholeness. Advances in Nursing Science 22, 16-32.

Estby, S.N., Freel, M.I., Hart, L.K., Reese, J.L., Clow, T.J. (1994). A delphi study of the basic principles and corresponding care goals of holistic nursing practice, Journal of Holistic Nursing, Vol. 12 No. 4, December, 402-413.

Fortney, L., Luchterhand, C., Zakletskaia, L., Zgierska, A., & Rake, D. (2013). Abbreviated mindfulness intervention for job satisfaction, quality of life, and compassion in primary care clinicians: A pilot study. Annals of Family Medicine 11, 412-420.

Freel, M.I., & Hart, L.K. (1999). Holistic Nursing In Nurses's Handbook of alternative and complementary therapies. Springhouse, PA: Springhouse Corporation, 61-82.

Heffernan, M., Quinn Griffin, M. T., McNulty, R., & Fitzpatrick, J. J. (2010). Self-compassion and emotional intelligence in nurses. International Journal of Nursing Practice 16, 366-373.

Hines, M. E., Wardell, D. W., Engebretson, J., Zahourek, R., & Smith, M. C. (2015). Holistic nurses' stories of healing of another. Journal of Holistic Nursing 33, 27-45.

Jackson, D., Firtko, A., & Edenborough, M. (2007). Personal resilience as a strategy for surviving and thriving in the face of workplace adversity: A literature review. *Journal of Advanced Nursing* 60, 1-9.

Joy, W. B. (1979). *Joy's way: A map for the transformational journey.* New York, NY: Jeremy P. Tarcher/Putnam.

Kemper, K. J., Mo, X., & Khayat, R. (2015). Are mindfulness and self-compassion associated with sleep and resilience in health professionals? *Journal of Alternative and Complementary Medicine* 21, 496-503.

Kenny, G. (2012). The healers journey: A literature review. *Complementary Therapies in Clinical Practice*, 18, 31-36.

McDonough-Means, S. I., Kreitzer, M. J., & Bell, I. R. (2004). Fostering a healing presence and investigating its mediators. *Journal of Alternative and Complementary Medicine*, 10 Suppl, S25-S41.

McKivergen, M. (2000). The nurse as an instrument of healing. In B. Dossey & L. Keegan (Eds.), *Holistic nursing: A handbook for practice* (3rd ed., pp. 205-225). Burlington, MA: Jones & Bartlett Learning.

Neff, K. D. (2003). The development and validation of a scale to measure self-compassion. *Self Identity* 2, 223-250.

Olson, K., & Kemper, K. J. (2014). Factors associated with well-being and confidence in providing compassionate care. *Journal of Evidence-Based Complementary and Alternative Medicine*, 19, 292-296.

Raab, K. (2014). Mindfulness, self-compassion, and empathy among health care professionals: A review of the literature. *Journal of Health Care Chaplaincy* 20, 95-108.

Şenyuva, E., Kaya, H., Işik, B., &Bodur, G. (2014). Relationship between self-compassion and emotional intelligence in nursing students. *International Journal of Nursing Practice* 20, 588-596.

Slater, V. E., Maloney, J. P., Krau, S. D., & Eckert, C. A. (1999). Journey to holism. *Journal of Holistic Nursing* 17, 365-384.

Smith, M. C., Zahourek, R., Hines, M. E., Engebretson, J., & Wardell, D. W. (2013) Holistic nurses' stories of personal healing. *Journal of Holistic Nursing* 31, 173-187.

Swengros D., Herbst, A. M., Friesen, M. A., Mangione, L., & Anderson, J. G. (2014). Promoting caring-healing relationships: Bringing Healing Touch to the bedside in a multi-hospital health system. *Holistic Nursing Practice*, 28, 370-375.

Wardell, D. W. (2001). Spirituality of Healing Touch participants. *Journal of Holistic Nursing* 19, 71-86.

Zahourek, R. P. (2012). Healing: Through the lens of intentionality. *Holistic Nursing Practice* 26, 6-21.

Chapter 3

HOLISTIC AND ENERGETIC FOUNDATIONS OF HEALING

Foundations of Holism and Energetic Patterns

Conventional medical care is most often concerned with physical aspects of disease, injury, and recovery. However, healing and holism is a complex, individual process that involves more than the physical. It includes the emotional, mental, and spiritual as well. Healing and holism involve wellness, wholeness, and wellbeing.

As a contemporary approach to energy healing based upon ancient wisdom, Healing Touch is grounded in the holistic and caring theory of Martha Rogers' Science of Unitary Human Beings. This theory and approach support the facilitation of self-care, healing, harmony, and balance in both the patient and the practitioner.

Nursing theorist Martha Rogers developed a conceptual system for nursing science and healing in 1970 know as the Science of Unitary Human Beings (Smith & Broida, 2007). In this theory, humans are seen as irreducible wholes as energy fields that are engaged in mutual processes with environmental fields. These pandimensional, "non-linear and infinite" fields compose the universe. Given the extensive, limitless expanse of the field "time as a linear concept is no longer relevant." According to Rogers, the fields of human beings are open and may be "identified by patterns that change continuously and innovatively... [from] lower to higher frequency wave patterns...manifested as increasing diversity." The framework of Rogerian science allows for the investigation of energy healing in a way that has yet to be completely understood by contemporary science. Rogers viewed biofield therapies such as Healing Touch as "one of the tools of holistic practice" that would be emphasized in the 21st century.

The Human Energy System

Albert Einstein referred to these subtle energies as those which are known because of the effects observed, despite the lack of instruments to measure these fields directly. Concepts of electromagnetism were in this category of the unseen and immeasurable only 250 years ago. The effects of electromagnetism could be observed, but the energy itself could not be measured.

In terms of the electromagnetic aspects of the human body, electrical conductivity in the body works from the surface of the skin inward to the organs inside the body. All are part of the full-body living matrix needed for the communication necessary for life and physical function (Oschman, 2009).

The human energy system can be viewed as numerous energy fields working in concert to maintain fundamental biological processes. These fields include the biofield surrounding the body, multiple local energy centers concentrated in specific areas of the body, and energetic pathways that regulate the flow of energy within the body. Each of these categories of energy fields correspond with energy systems described in the ancient health traditions of cultures worldwide. For example, the aura refers to the biofield, the chakras of Eastern cultures refer to the local energy centers located throughout the body, and the meridians of traditional Chinese medicine are the energetic pathways. Additionally, each of these field concepts is supported by evidence from contemporary scientific research. What follows is a description of each of the field categories as components of the human energy system.

The Biofield

The biofield, sometimes referred to as the aura, has been proposed to be made up of bioelectromagnetic energies, such as the magnetic field generated by the heart, as well as subtle energies beyond detection with current technologies (McDonough-Means, Kreitzer, & Bell, 2004). The field serves as a complex network of information and regulator of the living system. Its functional attributes include coherence, entrainment or coupling, and resonance. This concept is contrary to a systems biology approach to living systems, in which genes and molecules in cells regulate health and wellbeing (Rossi, 2002). However, this systems approach rooted solely in chemistry does not fully explain how all of the reactions within an organism are regulated and coordinated. Thus, Lynn McTaggart (2002, p. 49) posed the following question: "If all these genes are working together like some unimaginably big orchestra, who or what is the conductor?"

The idea of an energy field or biofield that permeates all living things is one of the major concepts in energy healing therapies such as Healing Touch, and is rooted in ancient wisdom. This concept has developed and evolved over centuries, garnering scientific support. In the 1930s, Harold Saxton Burr (Burr & Northrop, 1935) measured an electrodynamic field involved in development of animal embryos. Electrical currents were established as being part of the process of wound healing by Becker in 1974. All of these ideas continue to be confirmed with new technologies (McCaig, Sangster, & Stewart, 2000).

According to Karagulla and Kunz (1989),

> The most important function of the etheric body is the transfer of life energy or vitality from the universal field to the individual field, and

Chapter 3

Healthy Biofield

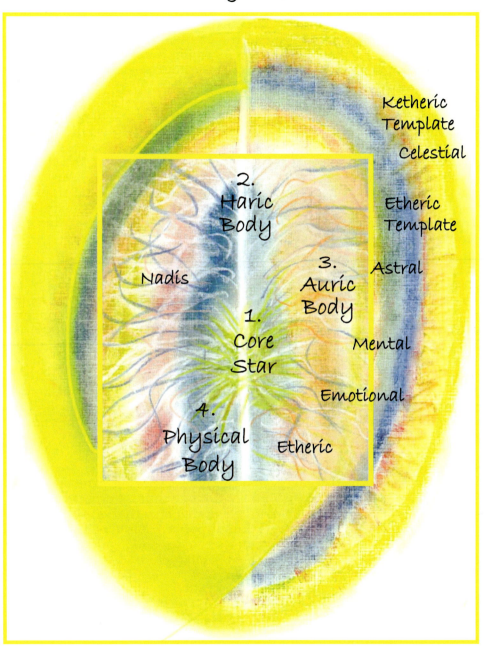

thence to the physical body. It is the primary contact with the ocean of life energy that sustains all of nature. Vitality is not recognized as a form of energy in the West, but in the East, where it is known as *prana*, it has always been perceived as a universal force in nature connected with breathing and breath...The etheric also acts as a connecting link between the physical body and the emotional and mental vehicles, although all of these are interpenetrating and synchronized, thus constituting, with the physical body, the instrument of the conscious self during the whole of life. (p. 28)

Healing traditions also espouse the concept of illness emerging first in the biofield before manifesting in the body. This, too, was confirmed by Burr, who found that specific pathologies corresponded with electrical characteristics of related organs, which were preceded by changes in the electromagnetic field (Burr & Northrop, 1939). The field can be conceptualized as having both electromagnetic and holographic properties that allow for the efficiency with which information is distributed throughout the body and the speed at which effects manifest during a Healing Touch session (Rubik, 2002).

The practice of biofield therapies such as Healing Touch involves changes in states of consciousness through healing focus and intention toward the patient. During states of meditation and mindfulness, such as healer preparation, the vibrations of molecules throughout the body harmonize and sync into more balanced frequencies (Movaffaghi & Farsi, 2009). As this happens, the effect is reflected in the biofield and thus, may influence the fields of others through energy exchange and entrainment. As shown in the figure on page 45, entrainment is facilitated through actions of the crown and heart chakras of the patient and practitioner, facilitating healing presence and repatterning of the patient's field. This process highlights the necessity of ongoing practitioner self-development and self care.

Shields and colleagues (2017) define the biofield as:
>...a luminous field of energy that comprises a person, extends beyond the physical body, and is in a continuous mutual process with the environmental energy field. It is a vital energy that is a continuous whole and is recognized by its unique pattern; it is dynamic, creative, nonlinear, unpredictable, and flows in lower and higher frequencies. The balanced human energy field is characterized by flow, rhythm, symmetry, and gentle vibration (p. 12).

As shown in the illustration on page 29, the healthy biofield is dynamic, multilayered, and egg-shaped, with the smaller end of the egg below the feet.

The **Etheric Layer** is the layer of the biofield closest to the physical body in both proximity and energetic function. This layer of the field represents a physical duplicate of the body that guides the formation of the physical body, forming the energetic grid on which the physical body grows. Embryos grow through the direction of energetic fields. For example, the human brain forms from the actions of radial glial cells extending out into space and sending electrical pulses for the formation of the brain along the scaffolding created by these cells (McCaig, Sangster, & Stewart, 2000). Brennan (1987) describes this layer as being structured with lines of bluish gray light, extending one-quarter to two inches from the physical body.

The **Emotional Layer** is the sum of our emotional experiences in life, including our feelings, emotions, and personality. It is associated with how we feel about ourselves and others. Brennan (1987) describes this layer as being less structured and cloudlike, with rainbow colors that extend one to three inches from the physical body.

The **Mental Layer** is associated with our thoughts and beliefs, as well as our visual images (Kunz, 1995). More structured than the Emotional Layer, Brennan (1987) describes the Mental Layer as being composed of yellow light in lines extending three to eight inches from the physical body.

The **Astral Layer** is concerned with our spiritual dimension in terms of our higher purpose and our connection with the Divine or Source. Brennan (1987) describes this layer as being unstructured, with rainbow colors extending two feet or more from the physical body. Other healers describe this as the intuitional or spiritual field that is inclusive of all subsequent fields, concerned with higher order, compassion, creativity, and healing (Kunz, 1995).

The **Etheric Template** serves as the optimal blueprint of the physical body. Brennan (1987) describes it as looking like "the negative of a photograph" with transparent lines on a background of cobalt blue. The Etheric Template extending one to two feet from the physical body, provides the energetic structure for the Etheric Layer. Burr found that the electrical field around an unfertilized salamander egg was shaped like a mature salamander (Burr, 1972), suggesting an energetic blueprint for an organism. The biofield holds information about an organism, transmitting this information in the same way as a holographic plate distributes information in a hologram (Rubik, 2002).

The **Celestial Body** is described by Brennan (1987) as being made up of "beautiful shimmering light, composed mostly of pastel colors." The light has a gold-silver shine and opalescence similar to mother of pearl that extends two to three feet from the physical body. The Celestial Body is less defined than the Etheric Template and is the emotional level of the upper spiritual layers of the field. The Celestial Body may be reached through transformational spiritual work or meditation. Brennan (1987) notes, "unconditional love flows when there is a connection between the open heart chakra and the open celestial [layer] (p.53)."

The **Ketheric Template** forms what Brennan (1987) describes as the outer shell of the egg-shaped biofield, providing an energetic boundary containing all of the lower layers of the field. Highly structured, Brennan describes this layer as being made up of gold-silver light extending two to three feet from the body, with a golden grid structure that supports the physical body and human energy system. In a healthy individual, cone-shaped light vortices located symmetrically around the edge of the auras act as valves that control the process of absorption and rejection of energy within the greater environmental field (Kunz, 1991).

The Chakras

The second major component of the human energy system involves concentrated energy centers located within particular areas of the body known as chakras. The chakras are vortices of energy described in yogic and other ancient healing traditions. These energy vortices spiral above and within specific areas of the body and interact with the biofield (Eden & Feinstein, 1998). Dr. Valerie Hunt (1978) found that specific areas of the skin on the body were associated with extremely rapid electrical fluctuations. These fluctuations corresponded to the locations of the chakras.

Physiological and psychological functions have been attributed to the seven major chakras (Eden & Feinstein, 1998) and are shown in the figure on page 33. At the physiological level, the chakras correspond with the organs in proximity to the vortex and have an impact on the health of these organs (Leskowitz, 2006). Additionally, the chakras are aligned with the major nerve plexi of the spinal cord (Leadbetter, 1927). At the psychological level, chakras are associated with specific experiences or themes, providing an energetic memory system.

The Meridians and Nadis

The third energy system within the body is the energetic pathways known as meridians in traditional Chinese medicine and nadis in yogic traditions of India as shown in the illustrations on page 34. The meridians are described in many healing traditions and are most commonly associated with acupuncture. Mummified bodies thousands of years old that have been found in Europe, South America, and Siberia display tattoos on energetic points of the body along meridians indicated in traditional Chinese Medicine to be used for the treatment of specific ailments experienced by the individuals in life (Dorfer et al., 1999). Recent research has made observations that are beginning to confirm the structure and function of meridians. Biophotons generated by the meridians light up under imaging conditions and are identical to the channels described as meridians found in ancient texts of traditional Chinese medicine (Schlebusch, Maric-Oehler, & Popp, 2005). Additionally, acupressure points along meridians have altered electrical resistance and conductance (Reichmanis, 1975).

In Indian traditions, nadis, a Sanskrit word meaning "flowing water," are subtle energy conduits or channels within the auric field. The chakras and nadis are part of the same system, with the chakras being the epicenters and origins of energy flow. The network of 72,000 nadis interconnect and

Chapter 3

Basic Physiological and Psychological Functions of the Major Chakras

CROWN CHAKRA
Element: Thought
Endocrine gland: Pineal
Related organs: Upper brain & right eye
Function: Connection to spirit, harmony, & joy
Common dysfunction: Feelings of alienation, confusion, depression, and disconnection

BROW CHAKRA
Element: Light
Endocrine gland: Pituitary
Related organs: Left eye, ears, nose, sinuses, & lower brain
Function: Insight, wisdom, compassion, & humor
Common dysfunction: Sinus headache & blurred vision

THROAT CHAKRA
Element: Sound
Endocrine gland: Thyroid
Related organs: Bronchia, lungs, & larynx
Function: Clear communication
Common dysfunction: Throat problems, bronchitis, & voice

HEART CHAKRA
Element: Air
Endocrine gland: Thymus
Related organs: Heart & circulatory system
Function: Sense of well-being & compassion
Common dysfunction: Cardiovascular disease, immune system, & unresolved grief

SOLAR PLEXUS CHAKRA
Element: Fire
Endocrine gland: Pancreas
Related organs: Digestive system
Function: Positive self-esteem
Common dysfunction: Addiction, digestive problems, diabetes, & lack of trust

SACRAL CHAKRA
Element: Water
Endocrine gland: Gonads
Related organs: Reproductive system
Function: Relationships & community
Common dysfunction: Fluid imbalance, & codependence

ROOT CHAKRA
Element: Earth
Endocrine gland: Adrenals
Related organs: Bones, spinal column, & kidneys
Function: Survival & security
Common dysfunction: Problems with low back or hips, fatigue, & lack of purpose

Adapted from Brennan, 1987; Dale, 2009; Judith, 1987; Karagula & Kunz, 1989; Leadbetter, 1927; and Slater, 1995

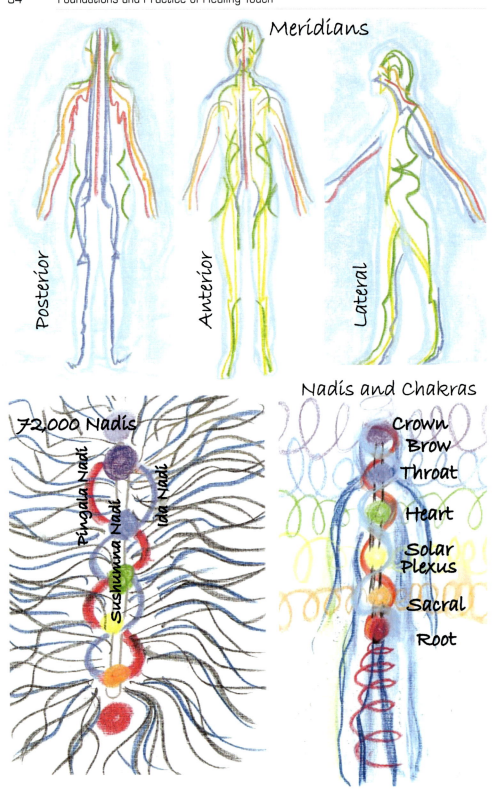

Chapter 3

Origination of the Four Energy Bodies

stimulate the seven major chakras, directing this energy flow. Primary nadis include the Ida nadi, a conduit of physical and emotional energy that flows downward on the left (female) side of the body; the Pingala nadi, a conduit of intellectual and mental energy that flows upward on the right (male) side of the body; and the Sushumna nadi, the major current passing upward through the spinal column that is the channel of kundalini.

The Four Energy Bodies

The human body and energy system can be thought of as consisting of four energy bodies: the Physical, the Auric, the Haric, and the Core Star (Brennan, 1993) s shown in the illustration on page 35.

The **Physical Body** is composed of the physiological structure of the body and is the most dense energy body in that it appears as solid matter. It is supported by the other three energy bodies.

The **Auric Body** consists of the biofield, chakras, meridians, and nadis. It is the sum total of the previously described human energy system.

The **Haric Body** is described by Brennan (1993) as being "one dimension deeper than the aura" or biofield, providing the structure on which the auric body is supported. It is named for the *hara*, defined by the Japanese as an energetic center of power within the lower abdomen. The Haric Body is comprised of three points or structures along the central line of the body: the individuation point, the soul seat, and the *tan tien*. This central line extends from a little over three feet above the head through the center of the body and down into the core of the Earth. The individuation point is a structure above the head shaped like an inverted funnel and associated with the point at which one individuates from the Divine. The soul seat sits in the upper chest and is described by Brennan as being composed of "beautiful diffuse light." The soul seat is associated with one's emotions and spiritual longing, the heart's desire that leads one through life. The third component of the Haric Body is the *tan tien*, a Chinese term referring to the center of power used in the practice of martial arts. Located a couple of inches below the navel, the *tan tien* grounds the haric line into the core of the Earth and can be a source of groundedness for healers. The structures and function of the Haric Body in healer preparation are further discussed in Chapter Four.

The fourth energy body is the **Core Star**, or one's divine essence. The Core Star is the source of life within, representing who one truly is and the divine individuality of the self. It is located just above the navel and exists beyond the limits of time, space, and belief. The use of the Core Star in healing and healer preparation is discussed further in Chapter Four.

References

Becker, R. O., Reichmanis, M., Marino, A. A., & Spadaro, J. A. (1976). Electrophysiological correlates of acupuncture points and meridians. *Psychoenergetic Systems*, 1(106), 195-212.

Brennan, B. A. (1993). *Light emerging: The journey of personal healing*. New York, NY: Bantam.

Brennan, B. A. (1987). *Hands of light: A guide to healing through the human energy field*. New York, NY: Bantam.
Burr, H. S. (1972). *Blueprint for immortality: The electric patterns of life*. Ashingdon, England: C.W. Daniel Company, Ltd.
Burr, H. S., & Northrop, F. S. C. (1939). Evidence for the existence of an electro-dynamic field in living organisms. *Proceedings of the National Academy of Sciences, 25*(6), 284-288.
Burr, H. S., & Northrop, F. S. C. (1935). The electro-dynamic theory of life. *The Quarterly Review of Biology, 10*(3), 322-333.
Dorfer, L. Moser, M., Bahr, F.,Spindler, K., Egarter-Vigl, E., Giullén, S., Dohr, G., & Kenner, T. (1999). A medical report from the stone age? *Lancet*, 354, 1023-1025.
Eden, D.,& Feinstein, D.(1998). *Energy medicine*. New York, NY: Penguin.
Hunt, V. (1978). Electronic evidence of auras, chakras in UCLA study. *Brain/Mind Bulletin*, 3, 1-2.
Karagulla, S., & Kunz, D. (1989). *The Chakras and the Human Energy Fields*. Wheaton, IL: Quest Books.
Kunz, D. (1991). *The Personal Aura*, Wheaton, IL: Quest Books.
Kunz, D. (1995). *Spiritual Healing*. Wheaton, IL: Quest Books.
Leadbetter, C. W. (1927). *The Chakras*. Wheaton, IL: Theosophical Publishing House.
Leskowitz, R. (2006). Energy medicine 101: Subtle anatomy and physiology. *Integrative Medicine Clinical Journal*, 5, 30-34.
McCaig, C. D., Sangster, L., & Stewart, R. (2000). Neurotrophins enhance electric field-directed growth cone guidance and nerve branching. *Developmental Dynamics*, 217, 299-308.
McDonough-Means, S. I., Kreitzer, M. J., & Bell, I. R. (2004). Fostering a healing presence and investigating its mediators. *Journal of Alternative and Complementary Medicine*, 10 Suppl, S25-S41.
McTaggart, L. (2002). *The field: The quest for the secret force of the universe*. New York, NY: Harper Collins.
Movaffaghi, Z., & Farsi, M. (2009). Biofield therapies: Biophysical basis and biological regulations? *Complementary Therapies in Clinical Practice*, 15, 35-37.
Oschman, J. (2009). Charge transfer in the living matrix. *Journal of Bodywork and Movement Therapies*, 13, 215-228.
Reichmanis, M., Marino, A. A., & Becker, R. O. (1975). Electrical correlates of acupuncture points. *IEEE Transactions on Biomedical Engineering*, (6), 533-535.
Rossi, E. L. (2002). *The psychobiology of gene expression*. New York, NY: Norton.
Rubik, B. (2002). The biofield hypothesis: Its biophysical basis and role in medicine. *Journal of Alternative and Complementary Medicine*, 8, 703-717.
Schlebusch, K. P., Maric-Oehler, W., & Popp, F. A. (2005). Biophotonics in the infrared spectral range reveal acupuncture meridian structure of the body. *Journal of Alternative and Complementary Medicine*, 11, 171-173.
Shields, D., Fuller, A., Resnicoff, M., Butcher, H. K., & Frisch, N. (2017). Human energy field: A concept analysis. *Journal of Holistic Nursing*, doi: 10.1177/089801016678709.
Smith, D., & Broida, J. (2007). Pandimensional field pattern changes in healers and healees: Experiencing Therapeutic Touch. *Journal of Holistic Nursing*, 25, 217-225.

Chapter 4

FRAMEWORK FOR A HEALING TOUCH SESSION

Introduction to the Framework for a Healing Touch Session

The framework used by health care providers to guide their care delivery is based on the scientific method, an interactive process used to explore observations and answer questions. The nursing process is a modified scientific method that was first described as a four-stage process by Ida Jean Orlando in 1961 (Orlando, 1961). This systematic, dynamic, assertive process is a problem-solving approach to the identification and treatment of a patient's physical, psychological, sociocultural, spiritual, economic, and lifestyle problems, which affect health. Necessary cognitive skills include critical thinking, problem solving, and decision making based on systematic and scientifically based theories and applications (Seaback, 2013). This framework includes the four steps of assessment, planning, intervention, and evaluation (Orlando, 1961).

The energy-based practitioner certificate program, that teaches the biofield modality Healing Touch, is a nursing continuing education program. The nursing process, a cyclical, ongoing, dynamic, goal-directed, patient-centered, collaborative, universally applicable process that can end at any stage if the problem is resolved, is used with modifications as the framework for a Healing Touch session.

The four steps of the nursing process were redefined for the practice of Healing Touch, identifying a seven-step process to include a practitioner preparation step that moves the practitioner into therapeutic presence. When a practitioner is present, one can become interconnected with the patient, creating a heart-centered, caring environment that influences and shapes outcomes (Andrus, 2014). In addition, the problem identification (i.e., diagnostic step) was separated from the activity of collecting data, and the mutual short- and long-term goal-setting step was separated from the planning step. Combining the state of presence with the intention of highest good for the patient, in addition to the patient's goals, provides a foundation for the Healing Touch work in which the realms of possibilities are endless (Schwartz & Kagel, 2014). The framework for a Healing Touch session is supported by the concepts of transpersonal caring (Tavernier, 2006). Practitioners maintain a full, heart-centered presence with the patient, which increases trust and creates an environment that supports the patient's self-healing process (McKivergen, 2000). This relationship is based upon Hildegard Peplau's theory of Interpersonal Relations in Nursing from 1951 (Peplau, 1951), which explains the therapeutic art of healing.

The following is a discussion of the framework for a Healing Touch Session, which is presented in the figure on page 44.

Practitioner Preparation: Healing Touch uses a heart-centered, caring relationship in which the practitioner and patient energetically align to facilitate the patient's healing. The practitioner achieves this relationship by moving into therapeutic (healing) presence through the activities of centering, grounding, attuning to the patient's field, and setting intention. Presence is a frame of mind rather than orientation toward action as in intention. Healing presence may emanate from a healer but requires some level of interaction with the patient for its ultimate effects on health and well-being. Presence is regarded as both a quality of and an intervention in healing (Tavernier, 2006). The concept of Presence is supported by several nursing theories and, as a term, has origins in philosophy and religion. Presence involves intentionality, mutual respect, patient focus, heart-centeredness, and authenticity.

Centering: The heart chakra is the locus where the act of centering is sustained, so that all aspects of the work are expressed through the heart chakra via the human attributes of love and compassion (Kunz, 2004a). The practitioner centers through the directing of awareness inward and operating from heart-centered decisions as evidenced by the presence of caring and compassion (Freel & Hart, 1999).

Grounding: The practitioner, with eyes open, becomes present in the third dimension (here and now) by focusing on and connecting with the Earth's energy, becoming entrained in the Schumann waves of the planet (Oschman, 2000). The electrical rhythms of the Earth have direct effects on the pineal gland, which is associated with the crown chakra and is the body's largest magnetoreceptor (Oschman, 2008). This neuroendocrine gland serves as a transducer, converting and intoning environmental signals of light, sound, temperature, magnetism, and electrical variations into neuroendocrine output throughout the body. By connecting the body to the Earth, the body becomes insulated from ambient electrical fields, offering a protective and stabilizing effect that decreases stress and tension (Oschman, 2008). This shift in autonomic balance through grounding aids the practitioner in remaining in healing presence.

Attunement to the patient's field: Attunement is the process of harmonizing vibrations and connecting energetically with the patient by moving into their field (Oschman, 2000; Watson, 2005). Patients may sync with the meditative state of the practitioner during this process through entrainment (Pierce, 2007). The magnetic field generated by the heart is the largest of any in the body. A practitioner who is grounded and fully present has an expanded, more balanced field through one's heart chakra. This balanced field can be picked up by the pineal gland of the patient. In fact, one's electrocardiogram (ECG), or heart wave pattern, can be registered in another person's electroencephalogram (EEG), or brain wave pattern (Oschman, 2009). Because of the strength of the practitioner's heart field by virtue of its size and frequency, the EEG pattern of the patient can be modified or entrained to that of the practitioner's heart wave pattern, bringing the two into synchronicity, as shown in the figure on page 45.

Intention: Intention, a key component of Healing Touch, is thought to initiate a flow of subtle energy that directly or indirectly influences desired outcomes (Bartlet, 2007; McTaggart, 2002). Intentions are thought-patterns that radiate out from a person in waves. The amplitude of the wave depends on the intensity of the pattern and is modulated by the degree of focus (Kunz & Peper, 2004). The effectiveness of the healer is dependent on the strength and clarity of the healer's intentionality (Kunz, 2004b). The intent of a Healing Touch session is always for the patient's highest good. Philosophically, intent is defined as a state of mind that is directed toward a specific action or set of actions. Awareness is projected with purpose toward an outcome. Through centering, grounding, and attuning, the focus of this awareness is honed into one of healing and allows for a stronger connection energetically with the patient. Intention allows for the communication between the energy fields of the practitioner and patient, assisting the practitioner in repatterning the field of the patient (Engebretson, 2002). Practitioners of Healing Touch, through presence and intention, hold a reference point of wholeness for the patient and their highest good through the head, heart, and hands.

Assessment: This action includes the collection of subjective, objective, and subtle energetic data related to the needs of the individual, family, and/or community, regardless of the presenting reason for the session encounter. These data gathering activities include the following: patient intake interview regarding the presenting problem; information regarding health and family history; observation of physical presentation and patterns (physical, behavioral, energetic); and observation of energy fields and centers using methods such as scanning with the hands, using a pendulum, or higher sense perception (e.g., visualization), as shown in the figures on pages 46-47.

Problem Identification: A conclusion or statement is made, based on the collected assessment data, regarding the patient's response to actual or potential health conditions or needs. The North American Nursing Diagnosis Association (NANDA-I) identifies descriptors for the diagnosis of "Imbalanced Energy Field" (Ladwig & Ackley, 2006, p. 325) as shown in the figure on page 48.

Mutual Goals: In collaboration with the patient, the practitioner addresses each identified problem, prioritizing according to severity and any potential to cause more serious harm, and determines which will receive attention first. Based on these decisions, the practitioner and patient set measurable and achievable short and long-term goals and outcomes related to each problem identified.

Planning: For each goal identified, a technique or set of techniques is selected that provides a rational basis for implementation in the present circumstance.

Intervention: Delivery or implementation of the techniques that were selected to help meet the established mutual goals is completed. Documentation of the techniques used and the subtle energy shifts noted during the interventions are included during this phase. Following the completion of the intervention and delivery of techniques, the **practitioner grounds the patient** by holding the patient's feet or shoulders. This gently brings the patient back into full awareness and connects them with the Earth. During the process of grounding the patient, the practitioner consciously releases the energetic connection with the patient and steps out of the patient's field.

Evaluation: Objective and energetic data noted and subjective data collected from the patient are used to determine the achievement of the mutual goal outcomes, recognizing that energetic changes may continue over the course of several hours post-intervention. New problems may be identified, as well as the rate of progress toward previously identified goals. "The real act of discovery consists not in finding new lands but in seeing with new eyes" (Proust, 1913). The need for referrals may be identified and documentation of the outcomes of the entire process completed.

References

Andrus, V. (2014). The scientific art of holistic practice. In D. W. Wardell, S. Kagel, & L. Anselme (Eds.) *Healing Touch: Enhancing life through energy therapy* (pp. 90-91). Bloomington, IN: iUniverse.

Barlett, R. (2007). *Matrix Energetics*. Hillsboro, OR: Beyond Words.

Engebretson, J. (2002). Hands-on: The Persistent Metaphor in Nursing. *Holistic Nursing Practice, 16*(4), 20-35.

Freel, M.I., & Hart, L.K. (1999). Holistic Nursing In *Nurse's Handbook of alternative and complementary therapies*. Springhouse, PA: Springhouse Corporation, pp. 61-82.

Kunz, D. (2004a). Beneficial influences on the chakras. In D. Kunz & D Kreiger (Eds.) *The spiritual dimensions of therapeutic touch.* (pp. 149-155). Rochester, VT: Bear & Co.

Kunz, D. (2004b). Chakras and the therapeutic touch process: Introductory comments. In D.Kuntz & D Kreiger (Eds.) *The spiritual dimensions of therapeutic touch.* (pp. 132-133). Rochester, VT: Bear & Co.

Kunz, D., & Peper. (1995). Fields and their clinical implications. In D. Kunz (Eds.) *Spiritual healing: Doctors examine therapeutic touch and other holistic treatments.* (pp. 213-261). Wheaton, IL: Theosophical Publishing House.

Ladwig, G., & Ackley, B. (2006). *Guide to nursing diagnosis* (2nd ed.). St. Louis, MO: Mosby, Inc.

McKivergen, M. J. (2000).The nurse as an instrument of healing. In B. Dossey & L. Keegan (Eds.), *Holistic nursing: A handbook for practice* (3rd ed., pp. 205-225). Burlington, MA: Jones & Bartlett Learning.

McTaggart, L. (2002). *The field: The quest for the secret force of the universe.* New York, NY: Harper Collins.

Orlando, I. J. (1961).*The dynamic nurse-patient relationship: Function, process, and principles.* New York, NY: G.P. Putnam's Sons.

Oschman, J. (2008). Perspective: Assume a spherical cow: The role of free or mobile electrons in bodywork, energetic and movement therapies. *Journal of Bodywork and Movement Therapies, 12,* 40-57.

Oschman, J. (2000). *Energy medicine: The scientific basis.* New York, NY: Churchill Livingstone.

Peplau, H. E. (1951). Toward new concepts in nursing and nursing education.*American Journal of Nursing, 51,* 722-724.

Pierce, B. (2007). The use of biofield therapies in cancer care.*Clinical Journal of Oncology Nursing* 11, 253-258.

Proust, M. (1913). *Nouvelle revue Francais.* Paris.

Seaback, W. W. (2013) Nursing Process: Concepts & Applications. Delmar. Clifton Park, NY.

Schwartz, G. E., & Kagel, S. (2014). Healing Touch International's intention experiments. In D. W. Wardell, S. Kagel, & L. Anselme (Eds.) *Healing Touch: Enhancing life through energy therapy* (pp. 98-104). Bloomington, IN: iUniverse.

Tavernier, S. S. (2006).An evidence-based conceptual analysis of presence.*Holistic Nursing Practice, 20,* 152-156.

Watson, J. (2005). *Caring science as sacred science.* Philadelphia, PA: Davis, Co.

Framework for a Healing Touch Session

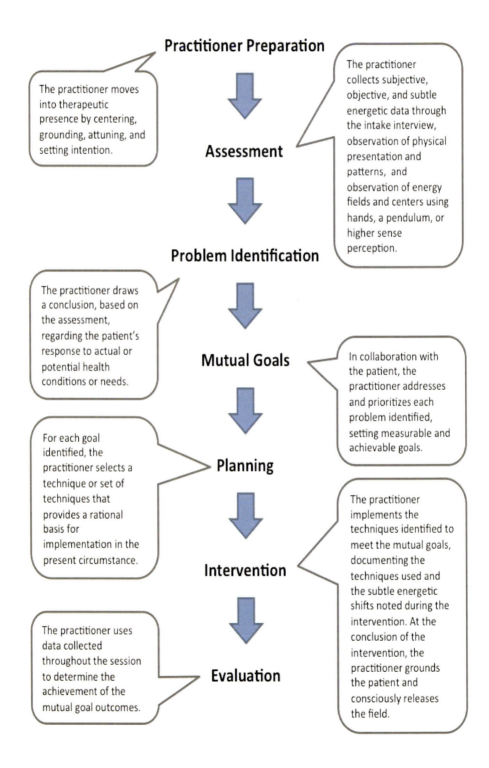

Chapter 4

Geomagnetic Entrainment & Grounding

Grounding and centering of practitioner involves connecting with the energy of the Earth.

The crown chakra is connected with the pineal gland, which is the body's largest magnetoreceptor.

Activation of Crown Chakra

Intention

Focused attention of the practitioner induces a meditative state that affects both practitioner and client.

The heart chakra is connected with the heart, which produces the body's largest magnetic field.

Activation of Heart Chakra Entrainment

Healing

Client entrains with the practitioner through the practitioner's heart field and subtle energies emitted from practitioner's hands have effects at the cellular and quantum level.

DO Post Assessment

Intake and Documentation Considerations

Topic	Items
Contact Information and Demographics	<ul><li>Name, Address, Phone, and Email</li><li>Date of Birth</li><li>Height and Weight (Optional)</li><li>Emergency Contact</li><li>Primary Health Care Provider(s)</li><li>Complementary Health Care Professional(s)</li></ul>
Purpose of Visit	<ul><li>Date of Onset, Duration, Description of symptoms</li><li>Changes/Progression/Evolution</li><li>Intensity/Severity of symptoms</li><li>Interference with activities of daily living (e.g., sleep patterns)</li><li>Tell me what was happening in your life when this started?</li><li>Have you ever had anything like this before? When? What was happening in your life then?</li><li>Who have you seen for this issue?</li><li>How are you managing this issue?</li></ul>
Overall Health? How would you rate?	<ul><li>Physical, Emotional, Mental, and Spiritual</li><li>Social and Cultural</li><li>Energetic</li><li>Other Health Concerns</li><li>History of Previous Health/Wellness and Illness</li><li>Current Medications and OTC medications/supplements</li><li>Exercise, Sleep Patterns, and Nutritional Support</li></ul>

Intake and Documentation Considerations

Topic	Items

Pattern Recognition	• Medical Diagnosis – Pathophysiology
	  • What are contributing factors that set the stage for this:
	    • Physical, emotional, mental, sociocultural, and/or spiritual
	    • Family history/genetics
	    • Previous injuries, traumas, surgeries, and/or illnesses
	• Energetic history
	  • Match up metaphors, archetypes, and field impressions
	    • Archetype references include Christine Page, Carolyn Myss, and Cyndi Dale

Subjective Data from Patient	Objective Observations	Assessment	Plan
Summary of the subjective information shared by the patient during the intake	Summary of the practitioner's observations and impressions during the intake	Conclusions and problem statements based on data and observations	Mutual goals and intervention(s)

Assessing and Describing the Energy Field

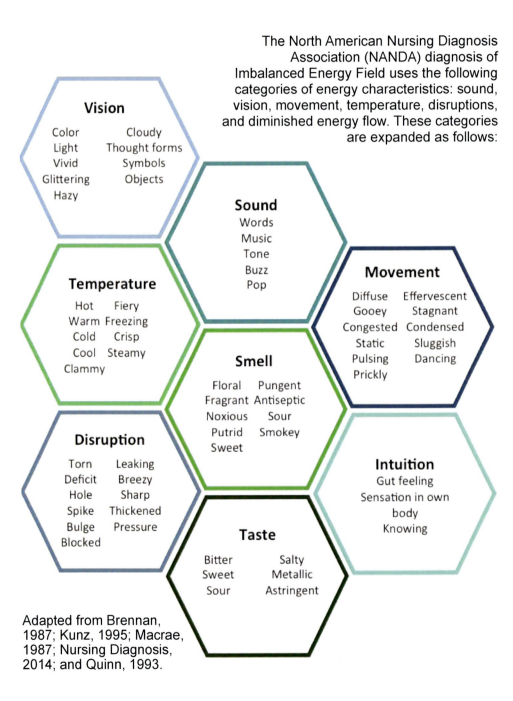

The North American Nursing Diagnosis Association (NANDA) diagnosis of Imbalanced Energy Field uses the following categories of energy characteristics: sound, vision, movement, temperature, disruptions, and diminished energy flow. These categories are expanded as follows:

Vision
Color, Cloudy, Light, Thought forms, Vivid, Symbols, Glittering, Objects, Hazy

Sound
Words, Music, Tone, Buzz, Pop

Movement
Diffuse, Effervescent, Gooey, Stagnant, Congested, Condensed, Static, Sluggish, Pulsing, Dancing, Prickly

Temperature
Hot, Fiery, Warm, Freezing, Cold, Crisp, Cool, Steamy, Clammy

Smell
Floral, Pungent, Fragrant, Antiseptic, Noxious, Sour, Putrid, Smokey, Sweet

Disruption
Torn, Leaking, Deficit, Breezy, Hole, Sharp, Spike, Thickened, Bulge, Pressure, Blocked

Intuition
Gut feeling, Sensation in own body, Knowing

Taste
Bitter, Salty, Sweet, Metallic, Sour, Astringent

Adapted from Brennan, 1987; Kunz, 1995; Macrae, 1987; Nursing Diagnosis, 2014; and Quinn, 1993.

Chapter 4

ADVANCED HEALING SESSION

Healing Touch techniques may be combined in a variety of ways to address problems and issues presented by a patient to meet mutual goals. When a healing session involves working in the fifth (Etheric Template), sixth (Celestial), and seventh (Ketheric Template) layers of the biofield, this is known as an advanced healing session. This sequence clears, balances, and energizes the entire field, and requires the practitioner to use advanced healer preparation exercises prior to beginning the session. An advanced healing session is not something that a practitioner will use every day; a clear rationale should be developed for using the sequence based on information gathered from the assessment and intake. Given the level of practice involved and the layers of the biofield touched during the session, this sequence is often experienced by patients, as well as practitioners, as transcendent. The figure on page 50 illustrates the sequence used during an advanced healing session.

ADVANCED HEALER PREPARATION

In addition to the basic healer preparation steps (centering and grounding) described earlier in this chapter, advanced healer preparation is required when working in upper levels of the biofield that vibrate at higher frequencies. To be able to affect change at those levels for a patient, whether it be balancing, energizing, or clearing, one's own vibration must be clear and exceed the baseline vibration of the patient. By raising one's own vibration and energy level to a higher frequency, the practitioner is able to raise the patient's vibration to a higher, clearer state through entrainment. Techniques that require advanced healer preparation are indicated with a lotus symbol. Methods of advanced healer preparation include hara alignment, core star expansion, spinning the chakras, and etheric vitality meditation.

HARA ALIGNMENT

General Information

The following Healer Preparation cultivates healer energy, assisting in raising one's vibration, and increasing one's extrasensory perception and insight. It is particularly beneficial to use this healer preparation in combination with the Core Star Expansion and Chakra Spinning.

Hara is a term Japanese use when referring to the qualities of having strength, energy, and focused power in the area of the lower belly (Durkheim, 1975). It is viewed as a center of spiritual power. In the hara region of the lower abdomen is a central energy point called the *tan tien*. This point is the focal point of power in the hara and is referred to as the center of gravity in the body. The hara exists on the level of intentionality and has immediate correspondence with our intentionality as the auric field has with our thoughts and feelings.

A healthy hara line is located in the center line of the body. It is straight, well-formed, energized, and well-rooted in the earth's core. Each of

Advanced Healing Session

Advanced Healer Preparation

For a full spectrum healing session, advanced healer preparation is required.

The practitioner aligns their haric body, expands their core star, and spins their chakras in preparation.

Working in the 5th Layer of the Biofield

Following advanced healer preparation, Chelation is implemented.

Etheric Template Repatterning, Spinal Clearing, and Deep Auric Clearing may be used as needed.

Working in the 6th Layer of the Biofield

After completing work at the level of the Etheric Template, including use of any other techniques, Celestial Repatterning may be implemented.

Working in the 7th Layer of the Biofield

After completing Celestial Repatterning at the sixth level, Ketheric Template Repatterning is implemented.

Integration of the Healing Session

Following Ketheric Template Repatterning, no other techniques are used. The practitioner holds the space for the patient to allow them to integrate the healing session.

three points along the hara line are in balance, in alignment, and firmly connected to each other with a laser like line. The hara originates in a point that is three and a half feet above the head, which Brennan (1993) calls the individuation (ID) point. Through this point we have our direct connection to the god head. The hara line connects down through a point in the chest area called the soul seat, midway between the throat and heart centers. It is here that we carry our spiritual desires. The hara line continues down to the *tan tien*, our chi source, located about two and a half inches below the navel. The hara line continues down from the *tan tien* deep into the center of the earth's core, connecting to the power source of the Earth and synchronizing our field pulsations with those of the Earth's magnetic field.

HARA ALIGNMENT EXERCISE

Breathe in and out. As your chest rises and falls past your heart center, gather the qualities of the heart: compassion, unconditional love, healing presence, innate harmony and service. Breathe these qualities down into the *tan tien*. Bring your awareness to the *tan tien* in the abdomen. Feel the power and heat there, infused with the qualities of the heart.

With your intention, breathe these heart qualities upon a light beam through the *tan tien* down into the center, into the heart of the Earth. Anchor this light beam into the Earth. Touch into the Core Star of the Earth. Gift the Earth these qualities of the heart: compassion, unconditional love, healing presence, innate harmony, and service.

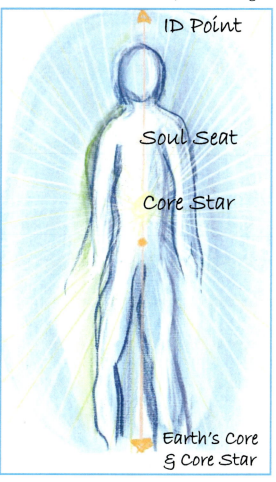

Bring your awareness back to the *tan tien*. Breathe a beam of light up behind the breast bone to the soul seat connecting it to the *tan tien*.

Bring your awareness to a point two to three feet above your head to the ID point. Breathe the beam of light connecting the Earth, *tan tien*, and soul seat up to the ID point, connecting with the ID point, moving onward into the heart of Source. You have now connected your heart to the heart of the Earth and the heart of Source.

CORE STAR EXPANSION

General Information

The following Healer Preparation cultivates healer energy, assisting in raising one's vibration, and increasing one's extrasensory perception and insight. It is particularly beneficial to use this healer preparation in combination with the Hara Alignment and Chakra Spinning.

Interior to the haric dimension lies your deeper core, the origin of your creative force, the internal source and expression of the divine. Here is the eternal essence of each person that exists outside of time and space. One can contact the essence of this core in the center line of the body approximately one and one-half inches above the navel. It emanates a brilliant light of many colors and can expand infinitely. Opening the internal corridor to our divine source, our core star, automatically connects us to love, truth and courage. This essential force in healing, automatically wells up through all four dimensions of our creative energy, expanding to permeate the essence of who we are. In the phase of expansion, a great deal of energy moves throughout our energy system. To complete this creative process through the experience of contraction, allow this essence to infuse and anchor throughout and within every cell in your body and acknowledge that which has been accomplished.

EXPANDING THE CORE STAR

Utilizing your breath, move your awareness to your abdomen, about 1 ½ inches above the navel, to a dimensionality deeper than the hara, to the core star, a beautiful, brilliant life that is the essence of your oneness with the Divine, or the Light. Acknowledge the harmonic with the Earth's Core Star.

Expand and radiate the core star in all directions as it moves through the auric field, through the Etheric Body, the Emotional Body, the Mental Body, the Astral Body, the Etheric Template, the Celestial Body, and the Ketheric Body.

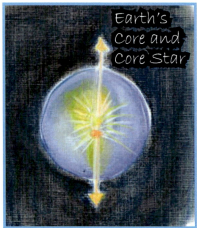

Earth's Core and Core Star

Bring the expansion into the physical body and the point of light radiating forth from every cell through every cell and its components. Let the core star shine forth through all levels of your being. Your entire being is an expression of your core star essence, of your Oneness with the Divine.

References

Durkheim, K. (1975). *Hara: The Vital Center of Man.* Sandpoint, ID: Morning Light Press.
Brennan, B. (1993). *Light Emerging: The journey of personal health.* NY: Bantam Books.

Chapter 4

SPINNING THE CHAKRAS

General Information

The following healer preparation cultivates healer energy, assisting in raising one's vibration, and increasing one's extrasensory perception and insight. It is particularly beneficial to use this healer preparation in combination with the Hara Alignment and Core Star Expansion.

In preparing ourselves as healers, we must first open and align with the light of Source. We must keep our body healthy in order to be able to raise our own vibrations to a level which aligns us with the healing energy needed to connect with the spiritual dimension. One can do this by visualizing the spinning of each chakra and allowing the body to move with the pulsating energy flowing through the energy centers. It engages the fiery, grounded energy of the Earth, to open, clear and charge all of our chakras and lift our energy up into the light of Source. Bruyere remarks that when we breathe deeply, we open to greater chi energy and life force. Consciously using our breath when we spin the chakras enhances the vitality of the flow, spin and the energetic charge of the chakras. (Brennan, 1987; Bruyere, 1989)

SPINNING THE CHAKRAS

- Bring your awareness to your **breath**. Easy in-breath; easy out-breath.
- Bring your awareness to your **feet** and their connection to the Earth.
- Imagine energy from the Earth entering the bottoms of your feet, coursing up through your legs into your hips and first chakra **(Root).** Begin spinning it clockwise (the clock is on the body facing outward). Breathe in red and breathe out red.
- Move to the second chakra **(Sacral)**. Begin spinning it clockwise. Breathe orange in and breathe orange out.
- Move to the third chakra **(Solar Plexus)**. Begin spinning this chakra, breathing yellow in and breathing yellow out.
- Begin spinning the fourth chakra **(Heart)**. Breathing in green and breathing out green.
- Move to the fifth chakra **(Throat)**. Breathe blue in and breathe blue out.
- Begin spinning the sixth chakra **(Brow)**. Breathe violet in and breath violet out.
- Begin spinning the seventh chakra **(Crown)**. Breathe in white and breathe out white.
- All chakras are now spinning. If we have established our hara line before spinning our chakras, they spin around an intact hara line.

References
Brennan, B. (1987). *Hands of Light: A guide to healing through the human energy field.* NY: Bantam Books.
Bruyere, R. (1989) *Wheels of Light: A Study of the Chakras.* Arcadia, CA: Bon Productions.

ETHERIC VITALITY MEDITATION

General Information *Go To Website for Meditation*

The following Healer Preparation cultivates healer energy, assisting in raising one's vibration, and increasing one's extrasensory perception and insight.

This half-hour meditation is based on the exercise suggested by the Greek mystic/healer Daskalos (1912-1995) to help cultivate a healer's energy. He advised that the exercise be done daily for a month to master etheric functions, or properties, and maintain the physical, psychic, and mental bodies in good health. This meditation serves a similar function as the Hara Line meditation - both cultivate healer energy, assisting in raising ones vibration, and increasing one's extrasensory perception and insight.

Etheric Vitality has four basic properties or functions: kinetic, sensate, imprinting, and creative. This meditation addresses three of these functions. **Kinetic function** (property) relates to the autonomic nervous system, movement of the circulatory system, lung, limbs, and metabolism. The **Sensate function** (property) relates to experience, feelings and sentiment. The **Imprinting function** (property) enables us to construct images through thought, telepathy, telekinesis. and exomatosis (astral travel).

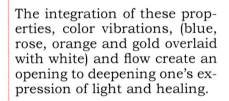

The integration of these properties, color vibrations, (blue, rose, orange and gold overlaid with white) and flow create an opening to deepening one's expression of light and healing.

The discussion of the meditation exercise suggested by Daskalos can be found in Markides, 1987, pp.58-60). A recorded reading of this exercise, used with permission and approved by the author, Kyriacos C. Markides can be found at www.HealingBeyondBorders.org in the student resource section.

Reference

Markides, K.C. (1987) *Homage to the sun: The wisdom of the magus of Strovolos.* London: Penguin Group Ltd. Arkana.

Chapter 5

HEALING TOUCH TECHNIQUES

Introduction to Healing Touch and Biofield Therapy Techniques

Healing Touch techniques have diverse origins, with many being rooted in ancient healing traditions. These traditions have evolved over time and contextualized into contemporary concepts of healing and care through the work of theorists, practitioners, and scientists. Techniques are presented in this chapter with general information describing the derivation of the technique itself, as well as definitions and applications in practice. The sequence of steps involved is presented, along with a rationale for each step and for the overall technique. While presented alphabetically, techniques are classified by the icons shown below, indicating whether the technique is used for balancing, energizing, and/ or clearing. Additionally, icons indicate techniques for which advanced healer preparation is required.

Clearing Energizing Balancing Advanced Healer Prep

CELESTIAL AND KETHERIC TEMPLATE REPATTERNING

General Information

The **sixth layer (Celestial Body)** is associated with celestial love. It is a love that supports caring and nurturing of all life. It is the emotional level of the spiritual plane. When we see love and light in everything that exists and feel we are oneness with everything, we have raised our consciousness to the sixth level. To heal on the sixth layer of the auric field, we work primarily through our heart, brow and crown. "You connect through the heart with universal love and then reach up with heart consciousness for the light" (Brennan, 1987). This heart consciousness enables us to hold the patient in our heart with total acceptance and positive regard for their well-being. Our consciousness goes up the spine and stretches into the white light.

The **seventh layer (Ketheric Template Body)** is associated with the higher mind, knowing, and integration of our spiritual and physical makeup. This golden template level contains the main power current that runs up and down the spine, nourishing the whole body. Work at this level restructures the seventh layer with gold light by cleaning and repatterning the grid structure of the organs, muscles, and other body parts, as well as the chakras. The spiritual guides' hands work directly though the healer's hands in an overlay manner. The guides overlay the shoulders and enfold the arms and hands of the healer. The golden light induces currents that circle the entire auric field, holding the whole field together.

The healing of the Celestial Body and the Ketheric Template is sequential. One immediately follows the other. However, before moving to this repatterning, complete a post assessment of the previous work done in this session.

Definition

Celestial and Ketheric Template Repatterning first involves the Celestial layer being infused with light and then the Ketheric Template is strengthened, balanced, and injuries, leaks and/or tears are repaired.

Application

Celestial Body and Ketheric Template Repatterning is used following Chelation and completion of fifth level work. We turn the work over to the guides for efficient healing. It is important in the cleaning, repair, and restructuring of the outer grid structure of the biofield and cleaning and restructuring of the chakras. It is invaluable following significant physical, emotional, mental and spiritual injuries and challenges to the energetic field and physical body.

Reference

Brennan, B (1987). *Hands of Light: A guide to healing through the human energy field.* NY: Bantam Books.

Chapter 5

HEALING OF THE CELESTIAL BODY

Implementation

Action	Rationale
1. Place your cupped hands in the etheric field over the patient's third eye, fingers together and thumbs crossing over each other forming a triangle.	Work on this level is through the 3rd eye and crown.
2. With your vibration raised, reach up for the light and let it flow through you into the central brain area of the patient.	Raising the patient's vibration
3. As the patient's aura fills with white - gold light, slowly raise your arms with palms facing down.	Bring the light through every level
4. If your arms get stuck as you encounter one of the layers, remain there until your arms begin to move up again.	Supports the guides' repair of problems at that level.
5. Move hands up through all of the subtle body layers to the Ketheric Template.	
6. Separate your hands, 6 – 8 inches, and hold them parallel above the patients head (about two feet, until there is a feeling of fullness –you may feel some pressure on your hands.)	Indication that layer is filled with light

HEALING OF THE KETHERIC TEMPLATE

Implementation

Action	Rationale
1. Bring hands back together, sending an arch of gold light over the body from head to foot.	
2. Slowly, in a sweeping motion, bring your hands down and around the aura, coming together again beneath the patient.	Enhances and strengthens aura.
3. If leaks or disturbances in the field are noted (your hands may stop) wait for repairs to occur and then continue to complete the circle.	Supports the guides' repair work.
4. When your hands come together beneath the table completing the circle, step to the side of the table.	
5. Gently extend your arms parallel to the patient's body and hold the aura until a smooth flow is noted.	Indicates completion.
6. Step back out of the field and allow the patient to return to conscious awareness prior to grounding.	Allows for uninterrupted integration of the work.

CHAKRA CONNECTION

General Information
Dr. Brugh Joy (1939-2009), an internist specializing in heart and lung disease, left his allopathic medical practice in 1975 to acquire a greater understanding of spiritual and psychic healing. His transformational process is journaled in the book *Joy's Way: A Transformational Journey* (1979). He includes in this book a number of exercises and techniques that support the energy flow. One of the techniques he named and described is the Chakra Connection.

Definition
A full body technique that establishes an interconnection of the chakras, opening a free and unencumbered balanced flow (Joy, 1979).

Application
Promotes relaxation and well-being; establishes flow post-trauma, such as chemotherapy, radiation treatment, surgery, bone fractures, and tissue injuries; promotes and maintains balance during daily life and life challenges, such as marriage, graduation, planned surgery.

Reference
Joy, W. B. (1979). *Joy's way: A map for the transformational journey.* New York, NY: Jeremy P. Tarcher/Putnam.

CHAKRA ENERGIZING

General Information
The Chakra Connection is a technique whose primary purpose is to establish the flow between the chakras. Chakra Energizing uses the same format as the connection, but while the chakras will be connected, the primary **purpose is to energize the chakras.** Therefore, rather than moving to the next position when the flow is free and unencumbered, hold each position while the energy increases in the chakras and then comes to a still point. The still point indicates that the chakra has been filled with energy. In addition to connecting and energizing those chakras addressed in the connection sequence, this technique affords the opportunity to include any minor chakra that would benefit. Such minor organ chakras could be the ovaries, testes, uterus, pancreas, liver, thyroid, and adrenals. Each of these minor organ chakras could be connected with its associated major chakra such as 2nd chakra with ovaries, solar plexus with pancreas or the solar plexus with the adrenals. This connects and energizes these organ chakras.

Following completion of the chakra energizing, <u>another option for energizing the minor chakras and organs</u> would be to (a) place one hand atop the other over the organ, or (b) place one hand above (anterior) and the other hand beneath (posterior) the organ. Hold until the energy comes to a still point.

Chapter 5

CHAKRA CONNECTION AND CHAKRA ENERGIZING
Implementation

Action (average minimum time = 15-20 minutes)   Rationale

Action	Rationale
In sequence, the minor chakras of the limbs and major chakras of the body are held using both hands. One hand is placed over the lower chakra while the other is placed over the one above it.	The technique is full body, moving from the feet to the head. Both hands are needed to establish the flow between the chakras.

When the flow feels free and unencumbered, the next connection can be made. The chakra connections are made in the following sequence:

1. Right foot to knee; knee to hip
2. Left foot to knee; knee to hip
3. Hip to hip
4. Root to Sacral
5. Sacral to Solar Plexus
6. Solar Plexus to Spleen
7. Solar Plexus to Heart
8. Heart to Thymus
9. Right hand to elbow; elbow to shoulder
10. Left hand to elbow; elbow to shoulder
11. Shoulder to shoulder
12. Thymus to Throat
13. Throat to Brow
14. Brow to Crown
15. Crown to Transpersonal Point (with left hand's palm facing away from the Crown)

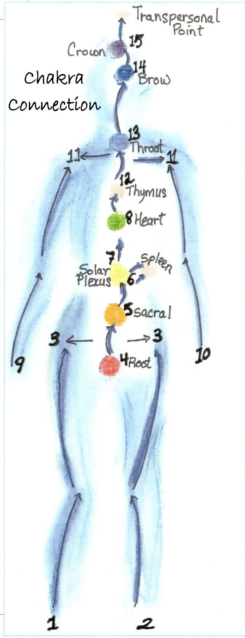

CHAKRA SPREAD

General Information

The Chakra Spread was developed by a hospice nurse who requested anonymity. She found that by spreading the energy of each chakra, the patient's field thinned and afforded increased ease in releasing from the field that which was no longer needed. This clearing of the field appears to facilitate transitions of all types. A practitioner in healing presence stays connected with the patient's heart center. The essence of the effect appears to emanate from expansion of the patient's heart chakra.

Definition

A full body technique delivered with hands off the body that gently and successively expands the energy of the chakras, thinning the patient's field allowing for release.

Application

Deep relaxation; facilitates movement between dimensions; eases physical, emotional, mental, and/or spiritual transitions such as changing jobs, moving, birth, marriage, divorce, graduation, and dying.

Reference

Kunz, D. (1995) *Spiritual Healing: Doctors Examine Therapeutic Touch and Other Holistic Treatments*. Wheaton, Il: Theosophical Publishing House.

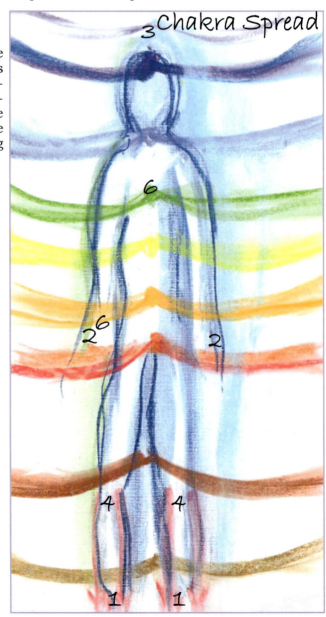

…

CHAKRA SPREAD

Implementation

Action (average minimum time = 10-15 minutes)   Rationale

Patient is supine.	Ensures safety of the patient.
1. Place palms of the hands on the sole and top of each foot.	Opens sole chakras to allow for ease of release.
2. Place palms of the hands into each of the patient's hands, thumb to thumb.	Opens palm chakras to allow for ease of release and connection with heart chakra.
3. Start at the head and move down the body spreading each of the following major and minor chakras in succession: crown, brow, throat, heart, solar plexus, sacral, root, knees, and ankles. Work ~ 4-6 inches above the body. Both hands held together, palms facing out and move them horizontally to gently spread the energy to the edge of the field. Repeat this spreading movement three (3) times at each chakra.	Each pass expands and thins the field. Gentle, slow movement without noise to avoid interrupting the process by jarring or abruptly affecting the patient's field.
4. Draw the gathering energy down from mid-calf with both hands then moving one hand above the foot and the other below the sole of the foot; continue off the foot. Repeat this movement three times.	Disperses accumulated energy from the lower legs.
5. Return to the head and repeat steps 3 and 4, two additional times.	
6. Hold one of the patient's hands palm to palm, thumb to thumb, and place your other hand over their heart chakra.	Signals completion and closure.
7. Move away from the patient and wait for them to arouse, continuing to observe the patient.	Remain with the patient for safety.
8. Ground the patient before assisting them to an upright position…OR	The patient may become very relaxed and ungrounded.
9. If the patient is to remain in bed, grounding is not necessary. Ensure that they are safe and secure.	Allows for deep rest and ensures safety.

CHELATION

General Information

Rosalyn Bruyere originated this technique to remove energetic debris from the auric field while filling and charging it with energy. Chelation utilizes practitioner grounding and an energetic push - pull activity, which claws out debris in the chakras and auric field. Bruyere begins this technique by taking a breath and running the energy from the Earth into the root and chakras at the bottom of the feet while drawing energy down through the crown chakra. The two energy flows meet in the practitioner's heart and are then directed out through the hands with the outbreath. The recipient's energy body draws in energy, which flows to where it is needed.

Effective use of this technique requires the practitioner to increase and maintain a high energy vibration. Immediately prior to initiating the technique, the process of spinning the chakras (Bruyere, 1989) and completing the Hara Line and Core Star Meditation (Brennan, 1987) facilitates the practitioner's moving to a higher energetic vibration where they can access the Universal Energy Field, to transmit, and transfer energy as needed (Bruyere, 1984).

Later modified by Barbara Brennan and other healing schools, the following implementation is a modification of Bruyere's and Brennan's Chelation techniques using modified hand positions from Joy's Chakra Connection (Joy, 1979).

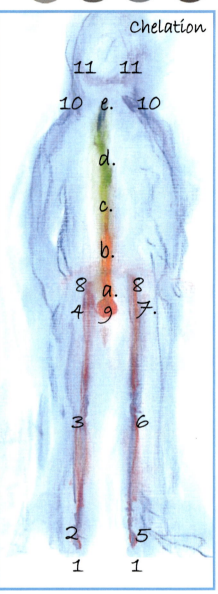

Definition

A full body technique used to clear, energize, and balance the first four layers of the field, raising the energy vibration of the patient to a level that allows work to be done in the 5th, 6th, and 7th layers of the energy field.

Application

Chelation can be used to address lack of progress in resolving compromised energetic patterns. It is necessary preparation for utilizing 5th level techniques and 6th and 7th level healing.

References

Brennan, B. (1987). *Hands of Light: A guide to healing through the human energy field.* NY: Bantam Books.
Bruyere, R. (1989). *Wheels of Light: A Study of the Chakras.* Arcadia, CA: Bon Productions.
Bruyere, R.L. (1994). *Wheels of Light: Chakras, Auras, and the Healing Energy of the Body.* NY: Simon & Schuster.
Bruyere, R. (2003). Returning the Healer Priest to Society, International Society for The Study Of Subtle Energies & Energy Medicine, "Return of the Sacred Science/ Celebrating the Mysteries of Healing" Conference, Boulder CO.
Joy, W. B. (1979). *Joy's Way, A Map for the Transformational Journey* NY: Jeremy P. Tarcher/Putnam.

CHELATION

Implementation

Action (average time=15 minutes)   Rationale

Action	Rationale
Throughout the technique, maintain a high vibration by spinning your chakras.	Allows entrainment of the patient's energy vibration to match the vibration of the practitioner.
With each hand position, send the energy from your lower hand (push) to your upper hand (pull) and hold this position until the flow is strong.	Indicates chakra is cleared and energized; it is time to move to the next position.
1. Standing at the foot of the table, place your palms on top of the feet, thumb on solar plexus point.	Balances right and left side of the body and field.
Move to the right side of the table. *Connect the following;* 2. Sole of foot to ankle 3. Ankle to knee 4. Knee to hip **(iliac crest)** *Repeat on opposite leg* 5. Sole of foot to Ankle, 6. Ankle to knee 7. Knee to Hip **(iliac crest)** 8. Connect the hips **(iliac crests)** 9. Connect major chakras on the torso (a. Root, b. Sacral, c. Solar Plexus, d. Heart, e. Throat)	
10. Hold the shoulders.	Balances right and left side of the body and field.
11. Stop your spin. Cup the cheeks.	Maintaining calm, compassionate presence.

DEEP AURIC REPATTERNING

General Information

The fifth layer is the template for all form that exists on the physical plane. If a form is disrupted in the auric field, it will have to be reestablished on the fifth layer of the field for it to regain its healthy form on the physical plane. When working on the fifth layer in a specific area, you can use both hands to enfold an area, you can "push" energy into an area with your right hand and pull with your left hand, or place both hands directly over the area penetrating and flooding new energy deep into the aura. You can also scoop and/or pull congested energy out of an area. The following techniques can be used to clear specific areas of congestion.

Application

Use following Chelation in situations where other pain management techniques have not completely reduced the pain. Also beneficial in situations where the energy is very blocked such as in severe muscle spasms or pain deep in a cavity.

Reference

Brennan, B (1987). *Hands of Light: A guide to healing through the human energy field.* NY: Bantam Books.

HAND CUPPING WITH TWO HANDS

Implementation

Action	Rationale
1. Cup hands together with thumbs crossing and palms facing downward, leaving no space between hands.	Assists in gathering and focusing energy deep into the body.
2. Direct energy into the area, vibrating your hands.	Knocks blocked energy loose.
3. Lift your hands, pulling the loosened energy out of the body.	
4. If willing, allow the guides to remove the energy from your hands.	Frequency and direction of flow may spontaneously change to clear the area.
5. Infuse energy into the area until the flow subsides.	Indication that area is cleared and refilled.

Chapter 5

PUSH/PULL WITH HANDS ON EITHER SIDE OF BLOCK

Implementation

Action	Rationale
1. Place hands on either side of the problem area.	
2. With right hand, push energy through the blocked area as the left hand pulls the energy.	Breaks up the congestion.
3. When resistance to the push/pull diminishes, infuse energy into the area until the flow subsides.	Indicates clearing and reenergizing is completed.

ETHERIC HANDS SCOOPING

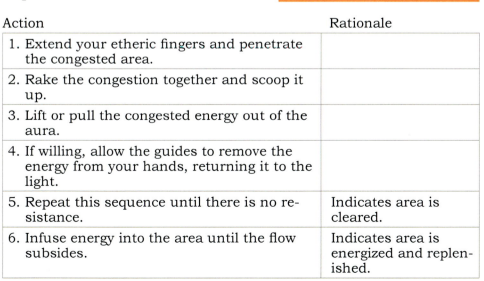

Implementation

Action	Rationale
1. Extend your etheric fingers and penetrate the congested area.	
2. Rake the congestion together and scoop it up.	
3. Lift or pull the congested energy out of the aura.	
4. If willing, allow the guides to remove the energy from your hands, returning it to the light.	
5. Repeat this sequence until there is no resistance.	Indicates area is cleared.
6. Infuse energy into the area until the flow subsides.	Indicates area is energized and replenished.

ETHERIC TEMPLATE REPATTERNING

General Information

Rod Campbell, a horseman and healer born in Whatatutu, New Zealand, in 1914, was able to support amazing and durable healing through his simple, uncomplicated approach to the pure expression of love, kindness, prayer, and respect for all living things. He would connect with the Divine in the ones who sought his assistance and then ask the Divine to send healing power through his hands. A warm glow would come into his hands and surround the healing activity. His hands would move through the field to the trouble, alternately drawing in and replenishing as he assisted the field to repattern. When healing, he visualized himself as a direct channel to the universal source of unity and love. The following technique is a modification of his work on repatterning in the fifth level to repair disruptions to the Etheric Template (energetic blueprint) and clear the Etheric Template grid.

Implementation

Action (Time = Determined by Circumstances)   Rationale

Action	Rationale
1. Scan the Etheric Template field.	To identify areas of restricted flow.
2. Starting in an area of restricted flow, begin moving your hands up through the Etheric Template.	Combing through all fields.
3. Move your hands, with soft palms up, fingers slightly parted, in a combing motion.	Parted fingers increase magnetic surface available. Congestion may feel like tangles.
4. When the problem area feels smooth, continue action until energy over the entire body in the Etheric Template is smooth.	Indication that disruptions and congestion have been cleared and Etheric Template is repatterned.

Application

Etheric Template Repatterning is indicated immediately following trauma, as well as chronic and acute conditions of any type, which have been unresponsive to previous work.

Reference

Campell, R, (1996). *Healing with Love: Healing through love, kindness and respect for all living things*. Auckland, New Zealand: Awareness Book Company, Ltd.

Chapter 5

FIELD REPATTERNING

General Information

Martha Rogers' conceptual system, the Science of Unitary Human Beings (Barrett, 1990), advances the three concepts of energy field, openness, and pattern. Living beings are energy fields open to the influence of other fields. A practitioner, whose hands move through a patient's field slowly and gently, assists one to repattern their field to an increasingly balanced state. According to Leadbetter (1927), the major energy flows are from the crown toward the feet, so that openness is addressed with repatterning upper areas first and then the lower areas of the body (Macrae, 1987). The practitioner's field may produce a voltage surge in the patient's field such that when hands are moved through the field, electrons may leap the gap in broken meridians, reestablishing the electric current and supporting repatterning of the flow in the field (Slater, 1995). When loosened congestion is not completely removed, the blockage can be released by holding the area, stimulating the energy flow (Macrae, 1987).

Definition
A technique that can be used to address the entire body or specific areas to assist in moving one's energy to an increasingly balanced state.

Implementation

Action (average time = limited by circumstance)   Rationale

When moving hands through the whole field:	
1. Move the hands through the field 2-4 inches above the body.	Work is done in the etheric layer.
2. Starting at the head, brush down and away from the body in a gentle and calming motion, sweeping and dropping any energetic debris out of the field.	The pattern of energy flow is from head to foot; movement returns the cleared energetic debris to universal energy.
3. Repeat these sweeps down the body to the feet until field is smooth and symmetrical.	Indicating the field is repatterned.
When addressing a specific area:	
1. Move the hands through the area above the disruption or blockage. If there is more than one area to address, begin with the upper ones.	The pattern of energy flow is from head to foot.
2. Move the hands close above the area using a gentle cupping and pushing motion.	To sweep away blockages.

Holding: Use after completing above activities	
1. Hold hands on or above the affected part of the body until the flow is reestablished.	To stimulate energy flow.
2. When addressing the entire field, place hands where convenient or where the patient directs.	Energy flows to area of need. Avoid the crown until your personal skill set and vibration are highly developed.

Application

Field repatterning can be used to address chronic discomfort or injury within specific areas of the body (e.g., shoulders, neck, or fingers). Can also be used on the whole field to break up areas of congestion seen with conditions such as depression, anger, anxiety, agitation, stress, burns, bites, pain, headaches, and nausea.

References

Barrett, E. A. M. (1990). *Visions of Rogers' science-based nursing.* New York NY: National League for Nursing.

Leadbetter, C. W. (1927). *The Chakras.* Wheaton, IL: Theosophical Publishing House.

Macrae, J. (1987). *Therapeutic Touch: A practical guide.* New York, NY: Alfred A Knopf, Inc.

Oschman, J. (2000). *Energy medicine: The scientific basis.* New York, NY: Churchill Livingstone.

Slater, V. (1995). Toward an understanding of energetic healing: Part 1. *Journal of Holistic Nursing,* 13, 209-224.

FIFTH LAYER HEALING

General Information

The fifth layer of the aura is called the Etheric Template because it contains all the forms that exist on the physical plane in a blueprint or template form. When the Etheric Layer becomes diseased, injured or disfigured, Etheric Template work is needed to provide the support for the Etheric Layer in its original template form. The form will have to be reestablished on the fifth layer of the field for it to regain its healthy form on the physical plane. It is at this fifth level that sound creates matter, so at this level sounding in healing is most effective. On the fifth layer, consciousness expresses itself as higher will, with which we manifest things into being through the power of naming and defining them. To bring conscious awareness to a higher level requires an increase in the vibrational frequency at which your awareness functions.

At this level your healing work begins to take place through intuition, knowing, and perhaps divine assistance of guides, teachers, or angels. Whether or not you chose to work with these beings is your choice. You can do quality work at this level without inviting the guides to assist you. You may intuitively be drawn to place your hands somewhere and led to keep them there until your hands feel free to move. If you ask and your guides decide to assist you with your work, you may feel their hands on your shoulders or on your hands, or you may see them or hear them, or simply feel that you are enfolded in a loving presence. Your patient may also experience the guides' presence and feel hands on their body in a place where your hands are not physically touching them.

Any technique can be used when working within the fifth level. However, the following techniques require a high vibration to be effective and are therefore considered to be techniques that are very appropriate for the 5th level work: the full body technique of Etheric Template Repatterning, and attention to specific areas with Spinal Repatterning and Deep Auric Repatterning techniques. Note: *After completing fifth level work, post-session energetic assessment is done before beginning 6th and 7th level interventions.*

References

Brennan, B. (1987). *Hands of Light: A guide to healing through the human energy field.* NY: Bantam Books.

Leadbetter, C.W. (1928). *Invisible Helpers.* Adyar, India:Theosophical Publishing House.

Leadbetter, C.W. (2000). The Inner Life. Wheaton, Ill: Theosophical Publishing House.

Leadbetter, C.W. (1978). *Man Visible and Invisible.* Wheaton, Ill: Theosophical Publishing House.

GLYMPHATIC SYSTEM SUPPORT

General Information

In 2012, researchers at the University of Rochester Medical Center discovered the "Glymphatic System", a previously unknown means of distributing the cerebrospinal fluid (CSF), a clear, colorless liquid that is continuously produced, fills, and surrounds the brain and spinal cord, lubricating and cushioning the brain against shock. The CSF also serves as the waste disposal and nutrient distributor throughout the brain. Formerly only known to move via the slow high to low gradient process of diffusion, this second system of movement operates through a highly organized, pressurized, fast acting CSF hydraulic delivery system that is managed by the brain's glial cells. These glial cells use "end feet" projections to form a network of channels encircling the outsides of arteries and veins inside the brain and are responsible for maintaining homeostasis, cleaning up debris, transporting nutrients to neurons, myelin formation, regulating content of the extracellular space, and providing protection for neurons in the CNS. *Central Nervous System*

Recent studies demonstrate the continuous interchange between the CSF and interstitial (between the tissues) (ISF) fluid. The collected debris from the CSF is moved into the ISF, where it drains out of the brain into the greater lymphatic system of the body through lymphatic vessels in the neck. During sleep, the brain cleans itself! The Glymphatic System functions primarily during sleep and is dormant during waking hours; it serves a similar function in the brain as the Lymphatic System does in the body. Amyloid beta, the protein that accumulates in the brain of patients with Alzheiemer's disease, owes over half of its removal to the Glymphatic System. "If the glymphatic system fails to cleanse the brain as it is meant to, either as a consequence of normal aging, or in response to brain injury, waste may begin to accumulate in the brain. This may be what is happening with amyloid deposits in Alzheimer's disease" (Iliff, et.al., 2012).

Kaminsky and colleagues hypothesize that brain degenerative diseases involve dysfunction of glial cells, resulting in pathological neuro-glial interactions. This in turn creates a hostile environment for neural cells, potentially leading to large scale systemic neural cell death and failure to defend against and clear oxidative debris produced during normal metabolism. This can create disruption of cellular homeostasis, undue cell loss, premature aging, and various types of malignancies.

A pilot study conducted at the University of Iowa Hospitals and Clinics on the use of Healing Touch in patients with Alzheimer's disease demonstrated significant improvements in cognitive function, mood, and depression in the treatment group, which is not typical of these patients. (Lu, Hart, Lutgendorf, Oh, & Schilling, 2013). The practitioners who carried out the treatments for the patients with Alzheimer in this study, consistently noted congestion in the groin, axilla and cervical areas, which they removed with energetic siphon and etheric hands. Therefore it would appear that if one uses this technique to assist in supporting the glymphatic system, the Lymphatic Clearing should be done first, followed by Glymphatic System Support.

Chapter 5

Definition
An energizing technique which supports the functions of the glymphatic system, which is to clear toxins and deliver nutrients.

Implementation
Action (average minimum time = 4-5 minutes   Rationale

Action	Rationale
1. Place palms at the base of the skull, fully covering the occipital ridge.	Energizing base of brain to support flow.
2. Place one palm on the occipital ridge and one palm on the brow.	Energizing and opening flow.
3. Cup palms gently over the brow and eyes.	Energizing and opening flow.
4. Place palms over the crown.	Energizing and opening flow.
5. Place palms over the temples.	Energizing and opening flow.
6. Place palms over the ears and sides of neck.	Opening flow and supporting interface between Glymphatic and Lymphatic systems.

7. to catch the energy and move it down the spine (cervical)

Application

When used in conjunction with Lymphatic Clearing accumulated toxins and wastes, and delivery of nutrients to the brain can support the brain in the following conditions: traumatic brain injury, inflammatory conditions of the brain and central nervous system, impaired cognition, premature aging, cancer of the brain, and sleep deprivation.

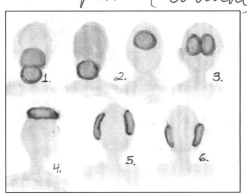

References

Lu, D., Hart, L., Lutgendorf, S., Oh, H., & Schilling, M., (2013). Slowing progression of early stages of AD with alternative therapies: A feasibility study. *Geriatric Nursing, 34,* 457-464.

Iliff, J., Wang, M., Liao, Y., Plogg, B.A., Peng, W., Gundersen, . . ., & Nedergaard, M., (2012). Paravascular pathway facilitates CSF flow through the brain parenchyma and the clearance of interstitial solutes, including amyloid beta. *Science Translational Medicine* 4(147), 147ra111.

Jessen, N.A., Munk, A.S., Lundgaard, I., & Nedergaard, M. (2012). The glymphatic System: A beginner's guide. *Neurochemistry Research, 40*(12), 2583-2599.

Kaminsky, N., Bihari, O., Kanner, S., & Barzilai, A., (2016). Connecting malfunctioning glial cells and brain degenerative disorders. *Genomics, Proteomics & Bioinformatics,* 14 (3), 155-165.

8. Take it down to Cervical spine down to base of spine

HOPI TECHNIQUE

General Information

The Hopi medicine men of the past used this method for adjusting the spine. The Hopi medicine man Grandfather David Monongya was Rosalyn Bruyere's teacher while she was on her journey of becoming a medicine woman of the Hopi, Navajo, and Cree Indian Nations. Rosalyn shared the Hopi technique with Rudy Noel when he attended a powwow at the Hopi Nation in Tucson, Arizona. A variation of this technique was also described in 1987 by Judie Chiappone RN, a Therapeutic Touch instructor, who also sources it from a Hopi Medicine man and reports receiving it indirectly.

Definition

The Hopi technique is applied to the spine utilizing hands to Laser, release, and energize the spinal area, allowing repatterning of spinal energy flow.

Application

Most spinal disorders and/or back pain to adjust the vertebrae and repair nerve damage.

References

Chiappone, J. (1987). *The light touch: An easy guide to hands-on-healing.* Lake Mary, FL: Chiappone Holistic Reflections.

Noel, R. (2011). *The Huggin' Healer.* Baltimore, MD: Publish America.

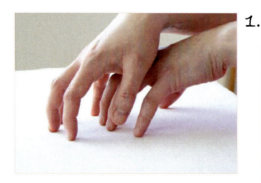

1.

2.

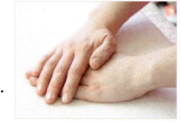

3.

Chapter 5

HOPI TECHNIQUE

Implementation

To determine the area of congestion or lack of energy flow in the spine, start at the neck. Assess each vertebrae via touching the vertebrae with one hand while holding the pendulum in the other hand.

Action (average time = limited by circumstance)   Rationale

Action	Rationale
1. Patient is in a prone position, and is encouraged to take easy, full breaths throughout technique.	Practitioner models breathing gently and fully throughout technique. Chi follows the breath and supports opening of flow.
2. Addressing areas that have indications of compromised flow, place **palms of hands, one atop the other**, directly over the spine of most severely compromised area.	Provides supportive energy to initiate flow in the compromised area.
3. Holding the wrists together, place the **finger tips on each side of the spine** and Laser into the area until pulsing occurs, then quiets.	Indicates muscles are softening and energy flow is reestablished.
4. Maintain contact with the body, shift the hands so that the **thumbs are on one side of the spine and all of the fingers are on the other**, forming a bridge. Laser into this area until the energy of the spine is felt in your palms.	Laser moves more deeply and penetrates the energy structures surrounding the spine.
5. Synchronizing your breath with the patient's, lift hands quickly up and then down. Hold hands in place until the energy flow becomes gentle and smooth.	To prepare for release of congestion. Breaks pattern up through the energy field. To cover, seal, and energize the area.
6. Reassess the spine with pendulum. If other areas remain compromised, repeat steps 2 to 5 in those areas	Open flow indication of repatterned energy.

9. The left thumb.

Do in Blue book
I might aula

LASER

General Information

Energy moves down the arm into the hands and fingers along the pathways of the following meridians: Large Intestine, Pericardium, Triple Warmer, and Heart (Tedeschi, 2000). This energy emanates from the tips of the fingers. The ancient practice of mudras utilizes this energy and its emanation from the fingers. Mudras that are useful in Healing Touch include the Prana Mudra or "Sword Finger(s)", to cut through ignorance and laziness and is used in martial arts to disrupt, cut, dissipate and direct vital energy, and Mukula Mudra, "Beak Hand" that is known to direct a laser ray of regenerating energy (Hirsch, 2000).

Definition

A beam of light or energy that extends from the fingers and is used to disrupt, cut, and/or dissipate blocked energy or to sew and bring energy back together.

Implementation

Action (average time = limited by circumstance)   Rationale

	Action	Rationale
1.	**Point** finger(s) at problem area holding hand steady.	For penetration of tissue.
2.	**Move** the tips of the fingers back and forth, changing angles. May use 1-4 fingers at a time.	To break up congestion. Using more fingers intensifies the energy extended.
3.	An alternative is **Beak Fingers Laser:** Gather the thumb and first two fingers (may gather all fingers) and continually move the hand in a circle or back and forth.	To soften the effect to reduce potential injury. Changing the angle of the Laser reduces the intensity. (Note: **Never direct stationary laser into the eyes or other fragile tissue**).
4.	When using the laser **to seal a wound or energy leak,** first determine how far out into the field the leak extends. Start at the point furthest from the body and using the thumb and first finger, or first finger only, use a sewing motion to bring the edges of the field back together.	The beam of energy at the tips of the fingers pulls together the edges of the separation in the field.
5.	After the field is together again, hold your hands over the area close to or on the body area.	Seals the reconnection by stimulating the area's energy flow.

Chapter 5

Application

Interrupts congested energy, such as found with the following conditions: sinusitis, inflamed tissues, edema, and muscle tension; seals or sews wounds or energetic leaks. Use Beak Fingers Laser near fragile tissues.

References

Chiappone, J. (1987). *The light touch: An easy guide to hands-on-healing.* Lake Mary, FL; Holistic Reflections.
Hirsch, G. (2000). *Mudras. Yoga in your Hands.* New York, NY: Wesier Books.
Tedeschi, M. (2000). *Essential anatomy for healing & martial arts.* Trumbull, CT: Weatherhill, Inc.

Sword Finger(s) Laser

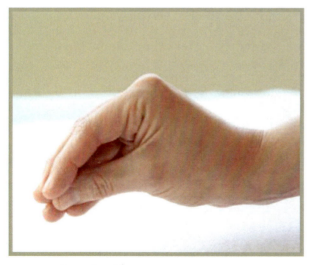

Beak Fingers Laser

LYMPHATIC CLEARING

General Information

The lymphatic system, composed of lymph, lymph vessels, lymph nodes, and lymphocytes (T, B, and NK cells), protects the body from fast growing cancer cells or foreign invaders such as pathogens. The lymphocytes are produced in the bone marrow; T cells mature in the thymus, B cells mature in the gut-associated lymph tissue, and NK cells mature in the bone marrow, lymph nodes, spleen, tonsils, and thymus. The lymphocytes are front line protectors. The lymph nodes, which exist in large numbers throughout the lymphatic system, filter the lymph, capturing and containing pathogens and other foreign invaders.

The lymph vessels begin in the extremities as microscopic closed ended ducts. They spread in a fine network, in close contact with the veins, throughout the body tissues. The lymph fluid contains the final by-products of metabolism that have been discharged from the cells: dead cells, blood corpuscles, and bacteria. These substances flow into the intercellular fluid, seep into the lymphatic capillaries, then flow onward into larger ducts. The lymph flow is transported by body activity and position, and muscle contraction as the system has no pump. The lymph eventually reaches larger ducts, such as the thoracic duct, which empties into the subclavian vein at the base of the neck.

The **head and neck** lymph ducts gather at a collection of lymph nodes in the anterior cervical region. The **arms and chest** lymph ducts gather in the axilla and the lower **abdomen and legs** lymph ducts gather in the inguinal areas.

The Lymphatic Clearing technique, using body position, energetically assists the flow towards the three gathering locations as well as toward the base of the neck where the lymph enters the Subclavian Vein.

This technique *may be utilized within either the Etheric level or the Etheric Template level (following Chelation)*. It can be done as a total body intervention or done only in a local or specific area, such as with an arm post-mastectomy. Completing the technique on the Etheric Template level enhances the effect.

Definition
A total body or a local area technique that supports clearing of the lymph system.

Chapter 5

Implementation

Action (time= average 5 -15 minutes)   Rationale

Action	Rationale
Note: *The patient lays supine with a pillow under their head and legs.*	Engages the effect of gravity. Also releases muscle and spinal tension.
With extended fingers and soft palms, the fingers are held about an inch just above the physical body.	Uses the effect of a Laser to break up the congestion.
Inguinal Nodes:	
1. Inguinal Nodes: Begin "brushing" up the legs toward the inguinal nodes in the groin. Repeat until resistance is no longer encountered.	Inguinal nodes are a gathering point. Flow is being reestablished. Indicates the lymph is clear and flowing.
2. Inguinal Nodes: Brush down the abdomen toward the inguinal area in the groin. Repeat until resistance is no longer felt.	Inguinal nodes are a gathering point. Flow is being reestablished. Indicates the lymph is clear and flowing.

3. Using one or all of the following techniques, **clear the inguinal node** area:
    Energetic Siphon
    Field Repatterning
    Etheric Hands
	Clears accumulated energetic debris within the nodes
	
	Note: **5th *level work requires Chelation***

4. *Repeat steps 1, 2, and 3 on other side of the body.*	
Axillary Nodes:	
5. Axillary Nodes: Move to the chest. Brush from midline of chest toward axillary region (arm pit). Repeat until resistance is no longer encountered.	Axillary nodes are a gathering point. Flow is being reestablished. Indicates the lymph is clear and flowing.
6. Axillary Nodes: Assist patient to extend arm up above the body. Brush from fingers toward axillary region (arm pit). Repeat until resistance is no longer encountered.	Enhances gravity effect. Axillary nodes are a gathering point. Flow is being reestablished. Indicates the lymph is clear and flowing.

7. Using one or all of the following techniques, **clear the axillary node** area:
    Energetic siphon
    Field Repatterning
    Etheric Hands
	Note: **5th level work requires Chelation**

8. Repeat steps 5, 6, and 7 on other side of the body.	
Anterior Cervical Nodes:	
9. Anterior Cervical Nodes: Move to the top of the head. Brush down to the chin, either one side at a time or both sides together.	Anterior cervical nodes are a gathering point.

10. Using one or all of the following techniques, clear the anterior cervical node area:
    Energetic siphon
    Field Repatterning
    Etheric Hands
	Note: **5th level work requires Chelation**

11. Repeat step 10, clearing activity at the base of the **patient's neck** on their right side.	Lymph empties into the subclavian vein on the right side of the chest.
12. Optional: If heavily congested turn patient over; repeat entire sequence on the **back**.	

Application

Lymph clearing is useful for lymphedema in the arms and/or legs; congestion or swelling in the abdomen; lung congestion with bronchitis, pneumonia, COPD; and congestion or swelling in the head such as sinusitis, head cold or with any chronic circulatory or metabolic disease.

Reference

Takaahashi, T. (1989). *Atlas of the Human Body*. Harper Collins Publishers, Inc.: NY.

Chapter 5
Lymphatic Clearing

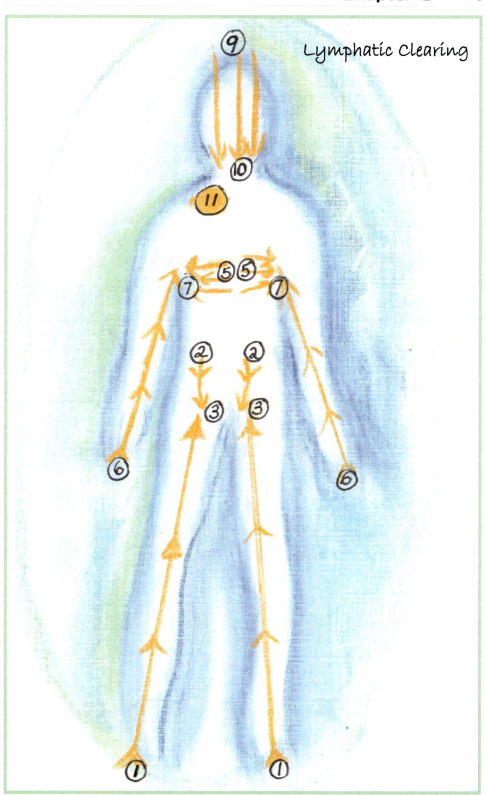

MODIFIED MESMERIC CLEARING

General Information

In 1773, Franz Mesmer, a German physician and surgeon, began using magnets for healing. His patients frequently noticed unusual currents coursing through their bodies. Mesmer discovered the same phenomenon could be produced by passing his hands above the body (Oschman, 2000). He found that deep relaxation, which the procedure produced with prolonged use, would move the patient to coma and allowed him to perform painless surgery prior to the discovery of anesthesia.

Definition

Modified Mesmeric Clearing is a technique for the entire body using the electromagnetic properties of the hands to clear congested energy and/or toxicity from the patient's field.

Implementation

Action (average minimum time = 15 minutes)   Rationale

Action	Rationale
1. Position hands parallel to each other with the fingers spread into the shape of claws, and thumbs close together.	Hand position increases contact with the field.
2. Drag hands slowly and smoothly through the patient's field about 3-6 inches above the body.	Decreased speed affords increased opportunity for the electromagnetic attraction over the entire length of the body in the etheric and emotional field.
3. Release the congested energy (which builds up in the hands), beyond the feet and out of the field.	Recycles energy to the universal field.
4. Repeat passes until the field feels smooth and free of congestion.	Indicates successful clearing of the field.

Application

Reduction of congested energy (1) that presents as pain (a) in chronic conditions, such as arthritis or chronic fatigue, or (b) acute conditions, such as surgery or bone fractures; or (2) caused by toxins, such as nicotine, alcohol, caffeine, drugs, anesthesia, pesticides, toxic chemical exposure, and/or unresolved emotions.

References

Oschman, J. (2000). *Energy medicine: The scientific basis.* New York, NY: Churchill Livingstone.

Esdaile, J. (1902). *Mesmerism in India and its Practical Application in Surgery and Medicine 1902.* Chicago, Ill: The Psychic Research Co.

Chapter 5

Modified Mesmeric Clearing

NOEL'S MIND CLEARING

General Information

The Mind Clearing technique was developed by Rev. Rudy Noel (Noel, 2011), a student of Rev. Rosalyn Bruyere who worked with Valerie Hunt, a professor and physician at the University of California-Los Angeles. Some of Rev. Noel's healing modalities included reflexology, massage, and hugging. Rev. Noel presented an experiential workshop on the connection between the heart and nervous system at the first Healing Touch International conference, in Lakewood, CO, in 1997.

Definition

A technique applied to the head that stimulates the parasympathetic nervous system, resulting in calming and deep relaxation. Patients are supported in energetically shifting into their high heart, allowing access to feelings of freedom, awareness, and forgiveness.

Application   *helps with Chemo*

Useful for stress reduction, ADHD, forgiveness work, stroke and aphasia recovery, blood pressure management, vision changes following chemotherapy, decision making, test preparation, public speaking, access of the all-knowing inner unconscious self, and facilitates clarity.

References

Noel, R. (1997). The Soul of Healing Energy. Charter Conference of Healing Touch International. Lakewood, CO.
Noel, R. (2011). *The Huggin' Healer*. Baltimore, MD: Publish America.

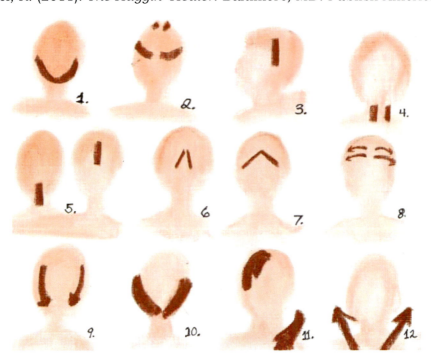

NOEL'S MIND CLEARING

Implementation

Action (average minimum time = 3-5 minutes)	Rationale
1. Cup hands under the occipital ridge, fingers on each side of the spine. Apply *gentle* pressure with fingertips.	Opens entire chakra system.
2. Cup the parietal ridge midway on the back of the head with fingers parallel and thumbs resting atop the fontanelle.	Normalizes blood pressure and connects with the heart.
3. Place the little fingers in the indentations above the ear and align the remaining fingers up the head toward the crown. Run energy between the hands until undulating energy is felt as a pulse in both hands.	Balances right and left hemispheres of the brain.
4. Place three fingers on either side of the larynx.	Balances thyroid and parathyroid.
5. Place fingers of one hand on the back of the neck (C2 to C5) and fingers of the other hand on the brow from the bridge of the nose to the hairline.	Connects hindbrain and cerebral cortex (helps reestablish impulse inhibition).
6. Place fingers of each hand on brow with little fingers at the inside of the eyebrow and the index finger at the peak of the hairline.	Influences inner sight.
7. Move little fingers of each hand to the outer aspect of the eyebrows, leaving the index finger at the peak of the hairline.	Influences physical vision.
8. Gently stroke across the brow, starting at the bridge of the nose to the hairline.	
9. Starting at the edges of the eyebrows, gently brush over the cheeks down to the chin.	Releases stress in the tempomandibular joint (TMJ).
10. Cup the jaw with fingers pointing toward the thyroid.	Relaxes the jaw and energizes area.
11. Place the left hand over the heart chakra and the right hand on the side of the head with the thumb pointing toward the crown.	Addresses pineal gland, pituitary gland and hypothalamus.
12. Place both hands over the heart chakra and brush from heart chakra up and out over the shoulders.	Gentle completion. Be mindful that hands are non-intrusive.

SCUDDER MERIDIAN CLEARING

General Information

Rev. John Alexander Scudder (1920 - 1995) was raised in Little Falls, NY. He held an Aircraft and Mechanic's license from the State Aviation School in Utica, NY, later working for Firestone, Goodyear Aircraft, and as an instructor at Thomastown Aviation School. Rev. Scudder served in the Air Force as a pilot and squadron instructor in WWII, later earning an Aeronautical Engineering degree from the Aeronautical University in Chicago (1948). An inventor, he held 17 patents. A devoted family man, he became an ordained minister in 1969, serving as pastor of the Christian Fellowship Church in Richton Park, IL, for 20 years, dedicating his life to others. A man of strong faith, he also had knowledge of metaphysical principles. He described levels of healing: one of loving one another; the second of magnetic healing of the aura; the third was healing of the mind through meditation; and the fourth was through miracle healing by placing one's hands on the solar plexus and raising one's vibrations to be one who touches the power and grace of God. During the last third of his life, Rev. Scudder was known to be a humble healer who worked tirelessly in the service of others, living what he preached (Shepard, 2001).

The Scudder Meridian Clearing technique, attributed to Rev. Scudder and similar to chi massage, uses a continuous, light sweeping motion along the meridians to remove excess or stagnant energy. The technique's purpose is to promote relaxation while the patient remains well grounded.

Definition

Scudder Meridian Clearing is a full body repatterning technique that addresses the meridian system, removing stagnant energy, reestablishing flow, and opening opportunity for healing.

Implementation

Action (time= 3-5 minutes)	Rationale
Patient may be seated, reclining, or supine. When moving to the back, a reclining or supine patient may either sit up or be turned to the side.	The technique is easily adapted to the surrounding environment.
Each of the following steps is repeated 3 times before moving to the next step. All sweeping action is to be done <u>gently and quickly</u> using the following sequence. When sweeping the limbs, the action always moves from the outer aspect of the limb, across the meridian, to the inner aspect of the limb.	Efficiently clears and activates the meridians. All of the following actions are following the flow of the meridians in the body part addressed.
1. Standing behind the patient, using both hands, quickly sweep across the forehead.	Sweeping away from the midline clears the central facial meridians.

Chapter 5

2.	With patients eyes closed, sweep across their eyes.	
3.	Sweep from the top of the head to down behind the ears, - giving ear lobes a tug.	
4.	**4A.** Palms cupping the chin, spreading index and middle fingers, sweep in front of and behind the ear then quickly up behind the ears and off the top of the head. **4B.** Gently press the acupressure points at the base of the occipital bone, then sweep up off the back of the head.	Activates multiple acupressure points in front and behind the ear. Activates acupressure points in the occipital area, called "Windows in the Sky" in TCM. Often blocked due to chronic tension and stress.
5.	Move to left side; while supporting the arm, sweep from the top of shoulder down to the inner aspect of elbow.	Opens and stimulates the meridians.
6.	Sweep from the outside of the elbow down the inside of the lower arm to the palm of the hand.	Opens and stimulates the meridians.
7.	Gently massage the hands and each finger, pulling congestion off its tip.	Releases congested energy and restores flow.
8.	Sweep congested energy out of the hollow below the throat (Suprasternal notch).	Common area for accumulated congestion.
9.	Sweep down the sternum and across the lower rib over to the side at the waist.	
10.	Sweep down from the outside of the hip crossing the thigh just above the knee, to the knee's inner aspect; sweep out energy from under the knee.	
11.	Sweep from outside the knee, across the shin and off the arch of the foot.	
12.	Massage the foot and each of the toes pulling congestion off their tips.	Releases congested energy and restores flow.
13.	Move to the right side of the patient and repeat steps 5-12.	
14.	Move to the back of the patient. Use short gentle motions, chopping across both shoulders.	Using Laser action to break up congestion.
15.	Sweep across and off the shoulders.	Assists in removing congestion and reestablishes flow.
16.	Reaching down to the tail bone area, sweep up the spine and off the shoulders.	

86   Foundations and Practice of Healing Touch

Application

Scudder Meridian Technique quickly calms agitation and hyperactivity in infants and children. Quickly reduces high anxiety in adults, yet keeps them well grounded. Useful with Jet Lag to reground and relax.

References

Shepard, C. (2001) *Back to Heaven*. NY: Writers Club Press.

Yasuo, Y. (Translated by Nagatomo, S., Hall, M.) (1993). *The Body, Self-Cultivation and Ki-Energy*. Albany, NY: State University of New York Press.

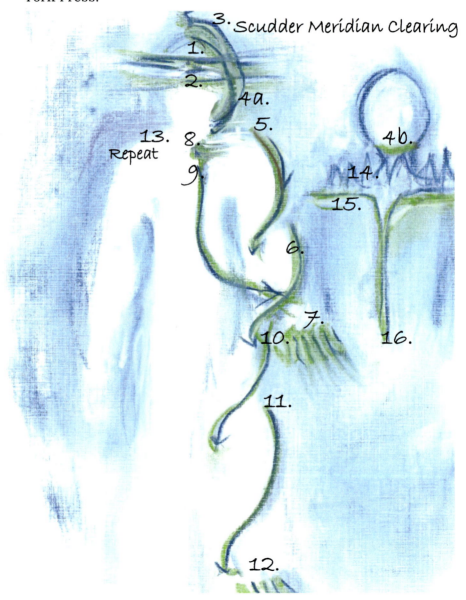

SIPHON

General Information

A siphon is a device that uses a gravitational pressure gradient to move fluid from one location to another. The energetic siphon is similar to the Pain Drain technique first developed by Rosalyn Bruyere (Bruyere, 1989) and can be used to move energy from one location to another.

Definition

An energetic siphon using the gravitational gradient to create an energy flow, draining or drawing off congested energy from a superior location to a lesser congested, inferior location.

Implementation

Action (average time = limited by circumstance)   Rationale

	Action	Rationale
1.	Place the left hand over the congested area.	The left hand is the receiving hand. The right hand is the sending hand.
2.	Place the right hand inferior to the congested area.	Uses gravity to accentuate the intensity of the flow.
3.	Pump the right hand as needed to start the flow and continue to sipon until the flow subsides.	Indication of gradient equilibrium.
4.	Reverse the hand positions and raise the left hand above the body.	Refills drained area with universal healing energy via the energy siphon mechanism.

Application

Siphon reduces congested energy, such as pain, edema, inflammation, infection, or emotional congestion, such as grief, anger, fear, and shame.

References

Bruyere, R. (1989). *Wheels of light.* New York, NY: Simon & Schuster.
Chiappone, J. (1987). *The light touch: An easy guide to hands-on-healing.* Lake Mary, FL: Chiappone Holistic Reflections.
Bradford, M. (1996). *The healing energy of your hands.* Freedom, CA: The Crossing Press, Inc.

Siphon

SPINAL CLEARING

General Information

Chelation will have cleared, energized, and balanced the first four layers of the biofield and will have cleared a healthy spine. However, if the patient has a spinal problem, the main vertical power current in their auric field may need to be cleared and reestablished on the fifth level for the spine to regain its healthy form.

Implementation

Action	Rationale
1. Patient is prone on a table with a face cradle.	Neck must be straight to allow for freedom of flow.
2. Locate the **foramen** of the sacrum (holes in the triangular shaped sacral bone through which the nerves pass.)	
3. Lightly massage, with small circles, the foramen areas on each side of the bone while sending energy through your thumbs.	Relaxes the muscles in the area.
4. Using **Beak Finger Laser**, circle up the spine while maintaining contact with the patient's body. Circle up, out and away from the spine.	
5. **Cup your hands** over the 2nd chakra in the etheric field and begin moving your hands in a clockwise circle.	Helps collect the congested area.
6. When you sense the flow of the energy gathering, using the clockwise circling movement, **travel up the spine**, moving all congested energy up and off the top of the crown.	
7. Repeat steps #2 through #6 at least three times until the flow through the main power current feels smooth and clear.	Indicates clearing has been accomplished.

Application

Spinal Clearing is useful with chronic and/or acute back pain due to injury or muscle spasms, spinal impairments such as scoliosis or spina bifida (myelomeningocele).

Reference

Brennan, B. (1987). *Hands of Light: A guide to healing through the human energy field.* Bantam Books: NY.

SPINAL FLUSH

General Information

Muscle tension is often the cause of discomfort felt in the back and neck. Whether the challenges a person is facing are on a mental, physical, emotional, or spiritual level, this approach will assist to calm them, balance their overall energy and help their energy to flow more effectively. The tension that people experience in their back is often connected to emotional issues, which not uncommonly relate to past circumstances. Louise Hay has identified past emotions, still present, related to areas of the back. Generally speaking, the lower back issues relate to financial insecurity, and powerlessness; the middle back problems relate to anger, guilt, bitterness regarding old hurts; and upper back issues involve fear, confusion, and feeling unloved (Hay, 2009). The use of forgiveness work is frequently also needed to help the biofield remain open and flowing. If one is not trained in emotional therapy, so that you can explore these insights, referral to appropriate practitioners may be needed so that the patient can address these psychological issues.

The following techniques can be used whether the back problem is an acute or chronic issue to 1) relieve the muscle tension and discomfort and/or 2) to identify the areas of spinal energy congestion that need to be addressed using the Hopi technique, and stimulates the lymphatic system.

The spinal flush stimulates the lymphatic system. Stimulating the neurolymphatic reflex points along the spine can help regulate the flow of energy to the lymphatic system. When lymph is flowing toxins are released, blood circulation is stimulated, as is the cerebral spinal fluid activating the nervous system. The spinal flush also clears the associated meridians as it cleanses the lymph system, and the Beak Fingers Laser used to stimulate the reflex points relaxes the small muscles along the vertebra.

Balancing the body's energy with a Chakra Connection and opening the energy flow up the spine before using the spinal flush increases its efficiency and effect. The spinal flow can be opened by using the magnetic effect of polarity (Stone,1986) by holding the right hand on the sacrum and the left on the neck until the energy is felt to be flowing smoothly up the spine. An alternative approach to opening the spinal flow is to cup hands under the occipital bone with the fingers on each side of the spine, separating fingers with an inch of space between each. Apply gentle pressure until the pulsing in the finger tips is symmetrical (Kunz, 2004).

Definition

The spinal flush stimulates the neurolymphatic reflex points along the spine that regulate the flow of energy to the lymphatic system.

Note:
*Before starting the spinal flush **assess the vertebrae** with pendulum to determine the areas of congestion or lack of energy flow. Have patient lying prone with neck straight. Stand on the left side of the patient. Starting at the neck assess each vertebra by either: (1) touching the vertebra with one hand while holding the pendulum in the other hand, or (2) holding the pendulum directly over each vertebra.*

Implementation

Action (time = 5-10 minutes)   Rationale

Action	Rationale
1. Place the right hand on the **sacrum** and left hand on the **neck**.	Opens spinal flow using polarity.
2. Using both hands and **Beak Finger Laser**, start at the neck, and address each vertebra down the back; circle 10-12 times away from the spine gathering energy in your palm.	Stimulates lymph reflex points and relaxes small muscles along the spine.
3. Draw this gathered energy in a straight line away from the vertebra to the outer edge of the back and gently release, as though you are pulling a **draw string**.	Gently disperses the congested energy away from the spine.
4. Repeat steps 2 and 3 as you proceed down the spine.	
5. **Vertebral Spread**: Return to the neck and placing 4 fingertips on each side of the spine alongside the vertebra, palms facing outwards, gently spread away from the midline to the outer edge of the back. Repeat x 3. Proceed down the spine.	Further disperses the congested energy and stimulates the neuro-lymphatic flow.
6. Sweep down the back from the shoulders to the feet with palms and fingers soft and open. Repeat the sweeping 2 more times.	Encourages energy flow.
7. Using the pendulum, assess the vertebra to check the openness of the energy flow.	Open flow indicates the area is cleared and energy is flowing.
8. If congested areas remain, the Hopi technique could be used to address the remaining congestion.	Problem may reside with the bones and not the muscles or lymph.

Application

Back pain due to muscles spasms, sprains or tightness. Swelling in the shoulder and/or lower back areas

References

Eden, D. (1998). *Energy Medicine*. NY: Jeremy P. Tarcher/Putman.

Kunz, D.(2004). Beneficial influences on the chakras. In D. Kunz, D. Krieger (Eds.)*The Spiritual Dimensions of Therapeutic Touch*. Rochester, VT. Bear & Company, pp.149-155.

Stone R. (1986). *Polarity Therapy* Vol. 1. CRCS Publication: Sebastopol, CA.

Spinal Flush

SPIRAL MEDITATION

General Information

During a meditation while in Findhorn, UK, Brugh Joy MD, received a vision of a technique that connected all major and many minor chakras in a single spiral pattern. Joy describes using this as a personal self meditation as well as a technique of an energy transfer sequence with a partner (patient, client) (Joy, 1979). This flowing geometric pattern is similar to the twisting, spiral pattern of heart contractions and the basic pattern of the DNA molecule, which is a modification of a spiral.

An illustration entitled *Theosophia Practica*, published in 1897 in the *Bibliotheque Rosicrucienne* (No. 4) by the Bibliotheque Charornac, Paris, was described by Gichtel and kept within a small circle of devotees. "It is noteworthy that he draws a spiral, starting from the snake around the heart and passing through all the centres in turn..." (Leadbetter, 1927). This is also described in *The Mystic Spiral* (Purce, 1974).

In the Middle Ages, the Fibonacci sequence was described by the celebrated mathematician Leonardo Pisano Bigollo, in a book on mathematics (Liber Abaci,1202). His book is remembered for two contributions: one, he brought the Hindu system for writing numbers to Europe, which became the basis for the modern Arabic mathematics system. Second, he asked The Question whose answer is a sequence of numbers, known as the Fibonacci sequence and the Golden Mean. This consists of relative proportions in the form of a spiral that is the basis for nature, human anatomy, art, classical theories of beauty, and proportion.

Definition

A full body technique that expands the vibration of the heart chakra and carries the essence of this chakra to the successive activation of all of the chakras in the spiral.

Application

Expanding the heart chakra enhances the healing effects of other techniques used in a Healing Touch session. This is also useful as a self meditation.

References

Joy, W. B. (1979). *Joy's way: A map for the transformational journey.* New York, NY: Jeremy P. Tarcher/Putnam.
Leadbetter, C.W. (1927). *The Chakras.* Wheaton, IL: Theosophical Publishing House.
Purce, J. (1974). *The Mystic Spiral, Journey of the Soul.* New York, NY: Avon Books.

Implementation

Note: **During self spiral meditation** – at Right Elbow Position, place opposite hand on right elbow. Flow travels in a spiral around the arms. At Right Hand Position, place opposite hand on right hand. Flow again travels in a spiral around the arms.

Action (average minimum time = 15 -16 minutes)	Rationale
1. Center awareness in the heart chakra.	Move into a heart-centered state.
2. Place hand over heart. When heart feels fully activated (1-3 minutes), repeat this process moving your hand in a clockwise sweep to each successive chakra in the following order: a. Heart b. Solar plexus c. Thymus d. Spleen e. Sacral f. Throat g. Root h. Brow i. Elbow (Left), Knees (using both hands) Elbow (Right) j. Crown k. Hand (Left), Feet (using both hands), Hand (Right) l. Transpersonal Point	Carries the essence of the heart chakra to all chakras.
3. If initiating a session with spiral meditation, use the session's Healing Touch techniques after spiral is open.	This technique prepares the field for deeper work.
4. Before closing the spiral, perform a post-intervention energetic assessment of the session.	Evaluates effects of other Healing Touch techniques used.
5. Close spiral by reversing the opening order by holding hand over the chakras briefly using a counterclockwise sweep (approximately 10 seconds).	

Spiral Meditation

Do this first to open everything

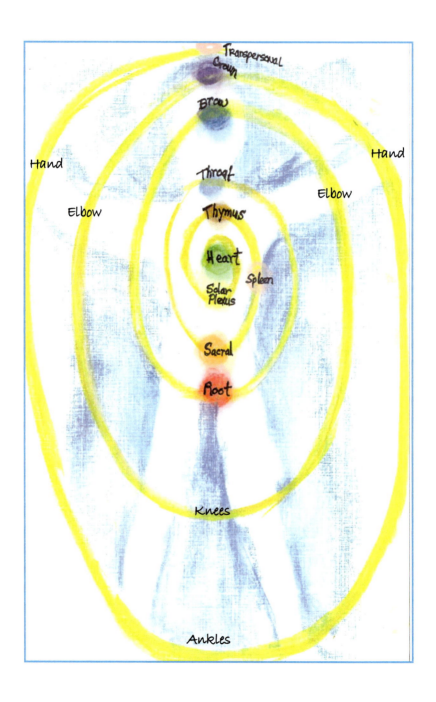

Chapter 6

ENERGETIC PATTERNS AND CLINICAL APPLICATION OF HEALING TOUCH

Healing Touch techniques can be applied in a variety of clinical and research settings in response to energetic patterns assessed by the practitioner. What follows is a discussion of the clinical applications of Healing Touch in general pain management and headache management, wound care and trauma, the evidence-based practice of Healing Touch from a research standpoint, and a brief overview of the use of Healing Touch in integrative health care.

Pain Management

A Cochrane Collaboration systematic review found that biofield therapies, including Healing Touch, are effective strategies for managing acute and chronic pain (So, Jiang, & Qin, 2008). Healing Touch has been shown to improve pain significantly in a variety of patient populations. Healing Touch is frequently used to manage pain experienced by patients with cancer.

Removal of a Pain Ridge or Pain Spike

Congested energy in the form of a block or ridge may form about 8 to 16 inches away from an injured area of the body. Such energy forms may be anywhere around the body and are usually found, with hand scanning, when the pain from the injury is not easily relieved with medication or an Energy Siphon. Such ridges not uncommonly accompany pain situations such as trigeminal neuralgia, fractured bones, whiplash injuries, sciatica, post operative, TMJ pain, and other joint pain caused by inflammation or muscle tension.

Congested energy may also be found in the form of a spike extending from an injured area with energy compression with the tip outside the body into the auric field. The usual site of a pain spike is the head where the brain is contained by bone. However, any area that is compressed, such as a hernia where the muscle contains or surrounds the herniated tissue, may exhibit a spike. A spike or multiple spikes are present with migraine headaches. A spike will extend outward from the head at the origin of the migraine pain.

To remove or reduce a **Pain Ridge**:

1. Starting at one edge or end of the ridge, use the hand action of **Field Repatterning**. *Gently*, using a hand over hand motion, smooth and cup out the congestion, clearing or sweeping it out of the field.
2. If the ridge does not easily dissolve, the use of a **Beak Fingers Laser** may help break up the congestion.
3. After the ridge is disrupted with use of a Laser, an **Energy Siphon** may assist in clearing the ridge from the field.
4. When the ridge dissolves, complete a full body sweep from head to feet, until the field is smooth and symmetrical.
5. Hold the hands above the affected area until the flow is reestablished.
6. Continually, during the above activities, ask for feedback from the patient regarding changes they notice.

To reduce a **Pain Spike**:

1. As with a pain ridge, **Field Repatterning** is used to reduce a pain spike. This is also addressed below in Migraine Headache.
2. *Gently*, using a hand over hand motion, leading with your palms, smooth and cup off the tip gently dropping or sweeping it out of the field.
3. If the pain intensifies, stop and take a step back away from the patient.
4. Restart the action when the patient is comfortable again.
5. When you are near the physical body, and the spike releases and dissolves, smooth the field and complete a full body sweep until the field is smooth and symmetrical.

Headache Management

Headaches are usually the result of energy congestion. **Laser, Field Repatterning**, and **Chakra Connection** can be used to shift and repattern the energy flow. Tension headaches are initiated by muscle tension in the back, shoulders, and neck that can extend up and over the top of the head. Sinus headaches result from congestion in the sinuses, which are located in the forehead, around the eyes, behind the nose, and cheeks. This congestion may be due to an infection, allergies, or environmental irritants. Migraine headaches result from vascular pressure in the brain, which can have many different locations. A person experiencing a migraine headache often is sensitive to noise, light, and movement. They may also experience nausea and vomiting as a result of the pain or the above noted sensitivities. A migraine headache can be treated during the headache, but all activities must be very gentle and slow. When the patient is not experiencing the pain of the migraine a shadow or pattern of the pain spikes will still be present around the head. This is one reason why persons who have migraines are uncomfortable when others move through their field. Treating a migraine involves the resolution of this spike pattern. Usually multiple treatments are needed to reduce and finally eliminate the migraine occurrences.

Chapter 6

Note: A sudden onset, severe headache warrants prompt evaluation by a medical professional as it could be heralding a cerebral vascular event (stroke).

Because each type of headache requires a different approach to treatment, it is important to verify with the patient what signs and symptoms are present with their headache.

To treat a **Tension Headache**:

1. Stand behind the person and with both hands using a four-finger **Laser** with fingers extended, breakup the energy over the upper back, shoulders, and neck. This can be done above the areas by moving the hand up and down through the energy or bringing the hands all the way down to the shoulders gently touching the body in those areas.
2. Brush off the shoulders, clearing the disrupted lasered energy.
3. Sweep up the back and across the shoulders, to clear the disrupted, lasered energy. Repeat this step until the energy is smooth and the muscles feel softened or relaxed.
4. Connect the 5th, 6th, & 7th chakras to provide an avenue for energy release.
5. Hold the left hand on the forehead and the right hand on the back of the neck to stimulate the flow of energy. The patient will feel a band across their forehead getting tight as the flow between the hands increases.
6. When the band on the forehead is tight have the patient, with a count of three, take a deep breath on 2 and blow out quickly and forcefully on the count of 3.
7. With the count of 3 quickly lift off your hands and begin **Field Repatterning** around the head and down over the shoulders.

To treat a **Sinus Headache**:

1. Use **Beak Fingers Laser** over the areas of the sinuses (forehead and cheeks) using a circular and/or back and forth movement. Continue Lasering until the patient experiences postnasal drip. When this occurs the patient will begin swallowing the mucous draining down into their throat.
2. **Connect** the 5th, 6th, & 7th chakras to provide an avenue for energy release and establish balance.
3. Hold the left hand on the forehead and the right hand on the back of the neck to **stimulate the flow of energy**. The patient will feel a band across their forehead getting tight as the flow between the hands increases.
4. When the band on the forehead is tight, have the patient, with a count of three, take a deep breath on 2 and blow out quickly and forcefully on the count of 3.
5. With the count of 3. quickly lift off your hands and begin **Field Repatterning** around the head and down over the shoulders.

To treat a **Migraine Headache**:

1. Identify the locations of the spikes around the patient's head. This can be done by:
   a) Asking the patient where they feel the pain during the migraine.
   b) Have someone watch the patient's eyes while you walk around them. They will blink when you walk through a spike and/or they may feel some discomfort.
2. **Field Repatterning** is used to reduce the spikes. Migraine headache spikes are often present in pairs, on opposite sides from each other when coming out of the head. When this is present. two people are beneficial to work on the spikes because as the end of the spike is gently smoothed away or cupped with the palm to reduce the tip, the opposite spike will begin to extend. The second person holds their two hands on the end of the opposite spike to prevent its extension. *(Note: If an assistant is not available, place energetic hands on the end of the opposite spike with intention.)*
3. If there are enough persons to help, place someone on the tip of every spike.
4. If the help is limited, work on the biggest or most prominent spikes first and utilize intention to gently hold the other spikes.
5. *Gently*, using a hand over hand motion, smooth away and cup off the tip gently dropping or sweeping it out of the field.
6. If the pain intensifies, stop the action and take a step back from the patient.
7. Restart the action when the patient is comfortable again. The paired persons alternate working on the spike they are attending.
8. As you approach the head and the spikes release and dissolve, sweep and repattern the field around the head until it is smooth. Follow by total body **Field Repatterning** until the field is smooth and symmetrical.
9. *Note: As an additional means to support the patient, instruct them in a form of "Quick Relax" technique, to imagine gently breathing (inhale, exhale) through air holes in the bottom of their feet. This assists in redirecting energy flow downward (Qi follows the breath) and expedites the clearing of the spike(s).*

Wound Care

Following significant injuries, traumas, surgeries or invasive medical procedures, not only the energy field within the physical tissues can become torn, cut. or damaged, this damage often extends through multiple layers of the energy field. This is indicative of an energy leak and is often noted during assessment as a flow of cooler energy through the field near the physically injured area. It is frequently noticed concurrent with a pain ridge and attempts to release the pain ridge are often met with persistent stream of cooler energy flow. It can be noted following acute injuries, as well as discovered following much older injuries. Tell-tale cues include persistent and chronic fatigue in the event of older injuries.

1. In the event of discovering a pain ridge and/or energy leak, use **Field Repatterning** as described above in Pain Ridge until the congestion is cleared. When the leak only extends into the etheric layer, use your hands to gather or scoop up the edges of the separated energy field and folding it over upon itself to close the area of the leak.
2. **Hold** hands on or above the affected part of the body where the energy has been folded upon itself, until the flow is reestablished.
3. In the event of an incision, older scar, or injury where the leak extends out into the layers beyond the etheric layer, use **Beak Fingers Laser** to suture the separated energy edges.
4. Start the suturing at the furthest out point where the leak is felt. It may be leaking all the way out to the 7th layer.
5. When the edges have been sutured all the way down to the etheric layer, gather and fold the separated energy onto itself and hold hands over the leak area until the flow has been reestablished. Finish with **Field Repatterning** over the area until the field is smooth and symmetrical.

Treatment of Head Trauma

A brain that has experienced a closed head trauma due to a blunt injury is very fragile and must be attended, during the acute phase, with very gentle, slow, smooth movements in the field. The goal of the work with a person whose brain has experienced closed trauma is to gently bring back the energy flow, to reconnect pathways and reduce discomfort. To assist the head energy to gently repattern to a normal flow place a hand over each shoulder by the ears, with palms facing up. The energy from each hand will flow up and over the head forming an arch. Allow the energy to be taken in as needed. When the energy flow stops or the energy is no longer taken into the body it is time to move on. If one placed their hands on and sent energy into the head the field may become overwhelmed in the enclosed skull. The field can be assessed with a gentle hand scan to determine whether there are energy leaks or a pain ridge. If so, these can be attended to with the appropriate application of an **Energy Siphon**, and the **Wound/Leak Closure Care**. **Field Repatterning** can be used to remove debris from the field helping to reestablish the flow around the head, neck, and shoulders. How close you can work to the head depends on the patient's comfort and may change when a pain ridge is removed or an energy leak sealed.

Evidence-Based Practice of Healing Touch

The current focus of health care is on evidence-based practice. Health care providers look for and incorporate into practice research findings that have been peer-reviewed. Evidence-based practice involves a systematic review of the available evidence and ranks this evidence in a hierarchical fashion. While several different ranking hierarchies are used in health care (e.g., Levels 1-4, Levels 1-5, or Grades A-E), all focus on peer-reviewed publications.

Conventional health care continues to rely heavily on evidence-based medicine and practice. In this case, the evidence refers to research results that are published in peer-reviewed journals. These journals rely on research experts in the field to review articles for accuracy, reliability, and validity of the methods used and results presented. Once published, this evidence is ranked using a hierarchy to rate the evidence. There are several different ranking systems that are used to rate the evidence. For a more in depth discussion of this topic, including how to rank individual research articles, please see the evidence-based practice chapter in *Healing Touch: Enhancing Life through Energy Therapy* (Wardell et al., 2014) and the Healing Beyond Borders *Research Brief*. To date, most published research studying the use of Healing Touch in clinical settings has been among patients with cancer, those with cardiovascular disease, or those experiencing pain (Jain & Mills, 2010; Anderson & Taylor, 2011).

Healing Touch has been shown to improve disease and treatment-related symptoms experienced by those with a diagnosis of cancer, specifically pain. Among patients with cancer who explore complementary modalities, biofield therapies such as Healing Touch are rated as providing the highest levels of benefit. Healing Touch complements the care received by patients with cancer by providing symptom management and improving quality of life. Healing Touch appears to improve markers related to immune function in patients with cancer. More research is needed to examine the effects of Healing Touch on other cancer-related symptoms, including fatigue and quality of life.

Healing Touch has been shown to significantly decrease the length of stay associated with coronary heart surgery. Healing Touch improves measures of well-being and quality of life in patients with cardiovascular disease. Biofield therapies have a positive impact on physiological measures related to cardiovascular disease, including heart rate and hematocrit levels.

Healing Touch has a significant, positive impact on measures of well-being and quality of life. Healing Touch has been shown to improve levels of mood, quality of life, and anxiety among patients living with chronic disease. Healing Touch elicits a significant relaxation response that leads to improvements in aspects of well-being and health, including mind, body, and spirit.

Healing Touch affects the energetic foundations of physiological processes, having an impact on the full spectrum of physical conditions. Healing Touch balances and optimizes the fields that surround, permeate, and support the body, both in terms of structure and function. In fact, these therapies can influence gene expression both directly, through activation of electromagnetic response elements in the promoter regions of genes (Oschman, 2000), and indirectly, through the psychoneuroimmunological framework of the relaxation response, which activates genes that decrease inflammation and promote immune function (Bhasin et al., 2013).

Integrative Health Care

The interest in and use of complementary and integrative health care continues to grow globally. These therapies provide options for populations with various chronic illnesses, as well as aid in meeting the mounting demands for personalized care. Given increasing patient demand, a growing number of hospitals and health care systems have begun offering integrative health care services over the past two decades. Patients are more involved in many aspects of their own health care, including decision making, and there is a growing interest in integrative health care as an adjunct to conventional allopathic care. Additionally, the expectations of society about conventional allopathic health care are changing, with people more inclined to seek out and use integrative health care, regardless of the cost, efficacy, or levels of evidence available.

Oftentimes, conventional allopathic medical care does not take a holistic approach to disease, focusing mainly on symptom management (Burr, 2005). Within the holistic health care paradigm, the person is viewed as a physical, emotional, mental, and spiritual being (King, 2005). This interrelationship and the relationship of the individual to the environment are significant factors in the healing process, with physical crises affecting emotional, mental, and spiritual aspects of health, and vice versa. Jean Watson's theoretical Transpersonal Caring Model concerns viewing the human being as a multi-dimensional system of energy, with a consciousness that can be affected by another to promote well-being. This model includes expanding the view of the individual to one of an energetic being composed of a spirit, universal mind, and consciousness (Parker & Lynn, 2006). The work of nursing researcher and theorist Martha Rogers suggests each human being is surrounded by an energy field that is in constant interaction with the environment (Parker & Lynn, 2006), with disruptions in this field manifesting as illness (Maville et al., 2008). Rogers advocated for the use of non-invasive modalities such as Healing Touch to promote healing on physical, mental, emotional, and spiritual levels (Parker & Lynn, 2006).

Healing Touch is used in a variety of health care settings, including hospitals, hospices, pain clinics, cancer centers, nursing homes, and private practices, and is administered by trained practitioners who are often health care professionals, especially nurses, to reduce pain, anxiety and promote health (Eschiti, 2007; Movaffaghi et al., 2009). Healing Touch fosters healing and prevents illness, as well as a stronger patient and practitioner partnership in the healing process. Healing Touch strengthens the integration of body, mind, and spirit, leading not only to a focus on healing, but to greater well-being and peace, promoting harmonious integration.

References

Anderson, J. G., & Taylor, A. G. (2011). Effects of Healing Touch in clinical practice: A systematic review of randomized clinical trials. *Journal of Holistic Nursing* 29, 221-228.

Barrett, E.A.M. (1990). *Visions of Roger's Science-Based Nursing*. NY, NY: National League for Nursing.

Bhasin, M. K., Dusek, J. A., Chang, B. H., Joseph, M. G., Denninger, J. W., Fricchione, G. L., Benson, H., & Libermann, T. A. (2013). Relaxation response induces temporal transcriptome changes in energy metabolism, insulin secretion and inflammatory pathways. *Public Library of Science One* 8, e62817.

Bradford, M.(1993). *The Healing Energy of Your Hands*. Berkeley, CA: Crossing Press.

Burr, J. P. (2005). Jayne's story: Healing touch as a complementary treatment for trauma recovery.*Holistic Nursing Practice,* 19, 211-216.

Eschiti, V. S. (2007). Healing touch: A low-tech intervention in high-tech settings. *Dimensions of Critical Care Nursing* 26, 9-14.

Jain, S., & Mills, P. J. (2010). Biofield therapies: Helpful or full of hype? A best evidence synthesis.*International Journal of Behavioral Medicine* 17, 1-16.

King, R. P. (2005). The integration of healing touch with conventional care at the Scripps Center for Integrative Medicine. *Explore* 1, 144-145.

Krieger, D.(1993). *Accepting Your Power to Heal: The Personal Practice of Therapeutic Touch*, Santa Fe, NM: Bear & Co, Inc.

Maville, J. A., Bowen, J. E., & Benham, G. (2008). Effect of healing touch on stress perception and biological correlates.*Holistic Nursing Practice* 22, 103-110.

Movaffaghi, Z., & Farsi, M. (2009). Biofield therapies: Biophysical basis and biological regulations? *Complementary Therapies in Clinical Practice* 15, 35-37.

Oschman, J. (2000). *Energy medicine: The scientific basis*. New York, NY: Churchill Livingstone.

Parker, M., & Lynn, C. (2006). Nursing Theories & Nursing Practice. 2nd ed. Philadelphia: F.A. Davis Company; 2006. http://www.R2Library.com/marc_frame.aspx?ResourceID=241.

So, P. S., Jiang, Y., & Qin, Y. (2008). Touch therapies for pain relief in adults. *Cochrane Database of Systematic Reviews*, Issue 4.

Wardell, D., Kagel, S., & Anselme, L. (2014). *Healing Touch: Enhancing life through energy therapy*. Bloomington, IN: iUniverse.

Chapter 7

PROFESSIONAL PRACTICE AND ETHICS

Healing Touch Code of Ethics and Standards of Practice

The following Code of Ethics and Standards of Practice guide the energetic and holistic practice of Healing Touch. More information can be found on the Healing Beyond Borders website (www.healingbeyondborders.org).

Definition: Healing Touch is an energy therapy in which practitioners use their hands to enhance and balance the physical, mental, emotional, and spiritual well-being of their patient.

Goal: The goal in Healing Touch is to restore harmony and balance in the energy system, facilitating the client's self healing process.

Code and Standard 1: Scope of Practice

Healing Touch practitioners integrate and practice Healing Touch within the scope of their education, training, current licensing, and credentialing. They represent themselves to the public in accordance with their credentials and practice within the guidelines of Healing Touch International's Scope of Practice statement.

Code and Standard 2: Collaborative Care

Healing Touch is a holistic therapy that is complementary to conventional health care and is used in collaboration with other approaches to health and healing. Healing Touch practitioners must know the limits of their professional competence. Health/medical conditions are to be followed by health care professionals. Referrals are made to appropriate health care professionals as needed.

Code and Standard 3: Self Development

Healing Touch practitioners work from a theoretical and practical knowledge base of Healing Touch. They integrate self care practices to enhance their own physical, emotional, mental, and spiritual well-being. They maintain a commitment to ongoing learning and self growth.

Code and Standard 4: Equality and Acceptance

The practitioner and patient are equal partners in the process of healing. Honoring individual autonomy, growth, and self empowerment, patients will be respected and valued at all times regardless of race, creed, age, gender expression, disability, sexual orientation, or health condition, honoring individual autonomy, growth, and self-empowerment, in keeping with the United Nations Declaration on the Rights and Dignity of Persons with Disabilities, which is recognized internationally by 160 countries. The Healing Touch practitioner respects the individual spiritual beliefs and practices of the patient. Healing Touch does not promote a particular spiritual practice.

Code and Standard 5: Communication and Education

Information given to the client is individualized according to the expressed need, context, and personal situation. The explanation about the treatment is conveyed at the level of the patient's understanding. Healing Touch practitioners act as a resource for appropriate education materials that can support the ongoing self care of patients.

Code and Standard 6: Healing Touch Process

The Healing Touch practitioner obtains essential health information, an energy assessment, and sets mutual goals. Appropriate interventions are applied, the energy system is reassessed, and patient feedback is obtained. This process serves as the foundation for understanding the health and healing needs of the patient and promoting patient safety.

Code and Standard 7: Intention

Healing Touch is offered only for the benefit of the patient, with intention for his or her highest good. The Healing Touch practitioner acts with the commitment to Do No Harm.

Code and Standard 8: Creating a Safe Healing Environment

Healing Touch practitioners provide a safe, welcoming, supportive, and comfortable environment that is conducive to healing. Consent for Healing Touch therapy and permission for hands-on touch is obtained. The practitioner is free from the influence of alcohol, recreational drugs, or prescription medication that would compromise their judgment, actions, or interfere with safe practice for the patient. The practitioner is physically, emotionally, and mentally capable of providing for the patient's care and safety during the entire Healing Touch session. The practitioner is dressed in a non-revealing manner, clean and professional in appearance, with a minimum of scent. The patient is empowered to give feedback, modify, or discontinue the session at any time. Safe and clear professional boundaries are maintained. Touch is non-sexual and non-aggressive and respects the patient's boundaries. The practitioner does not engage in romantic or sexual relationships with patients. The patient is clothed except in professional therapy contexts involving physical or medical interventions requiring disrobing, in which case appropriate draping is provided.

Code and Standard 9: Principle of Healing

Healing Touch practitioners recognize and honor the patient's unique self healing process. The individual is acknowledged as a complex being, who is part of a social system, and is interactive with and is acted upon by their internal and external environments.

Code and Standard 10: Confidentiality

Patient confidentiality is protected at all times. Treatment findings are documented appropriately specific to the practitioner's background and setting. Patient records are secured in such a way as to protect privacy and be in compliance with professional and legislative regulations. Patient written permission must be obtained prior to release of or reporting of any record or information.

Code and Standard 11: Quality Care

Healing Touch practitioners maintain a commitment to a high standard of quality care. The practitioner obtains supervision and consultation as needed from Certified Healing Touch Practitioners and other qualified professionals.

Code and Standard 12: Professional Responsibility

Healing Touch practitioners represent Healing Touch to the public in a professional manner by exercising good judgment, practicing with integrity and adhering to this Healing Beyond Borders Code of Ethics and Standards of Practice. (Healing Beyond Borders, 1996)

Ethical Practice and Professional Ethics

As Healing Touch students or practitioners, we may possess or be developing considerable skills and competence in balancing, clearing, and aligning the energy of our patients. Our patients, however, will observe, experience, and judge us by the way we demonstrate and practice personal clearing balance, integrity, and alignment within ourselves. They will know if our intention is to "Do No Harm" and they will energetically perceive whether we have created a safe environment that truly affords them respect and self-autonomy, one that supports their highest good and wholeness.

Professional ethics provides the framework for creating this safe environment. Health care professionals are held to ethical and practice standards that create that safe and highly professional therapeutic environment. While there are different systems for framing ethical action, in virtually all circumstances, it is the responsibility of the practitioner to establish and maintain such a safe environment within the professional relationship. The patient has the absolute right to expect that the physical, emotional, psychological, and spiritual environment within this therapeutic environment is always safe.

Many believe that by strictly practicing energy therapies, there is less need for vigilance due to the non-invasive nature of Healing Touch. In fact, the need for self-awareness, self-vigilance, and self-accountability is higher for those of us practicing energy therapies. When we connect energetically, boundaries blur and levels of knowing increase. Just by touching clients, we have already crossed acceptable social norms. Many clients are unprepared for the high level of intimacy that occurs within the therapeutic setting of energy work as we use gentle touch and unconditional love.

Because of the innate power difference within the therapeutic relationship, the patient may unconsciously recreate a relationship similar to one held with a former authority figure, such as a parent or boss. This is called transference, and in traditional psychotherapy, positive transference (e.g., "she reminds me of my favorite teacher") is actually important as it allows the client to have a sense that they can trust us as a practitioner. Practitioner-client relationships often recreate the parent-child relationship and any unresolved issues regarding that relationship. Our use of caring touch can potentially accelerate transference with the result being that the client may rapidly regress to a more childlike and vulnerable state. To further complicate matters, practitioners also carry unresolved needs and issues into the therapeutic relationship and may being to respond to the client as they responded to someone in the past, or even someone in the present. This is called countertransference, and if unrecognized and unchecked, can adversely affect the therapeutic relationship, resulting in diminished efficacy of therapy or even psychological harm to the client. When the practitioner has strong feelings about their patient (e.g., "the patient is just like my former..."), then it is time to seek outside help.

Healing Beyond Borders has held an international Code of Ethics and Standards of Practice for Healing Touch students, practitioners, and instructors since 1996. These codes and standards, described earlier in this chapter, serve to guide the energetic and holistic practice of Healing Touch. While striving for highest action and adherence to these guidelines, one of the most common ethical challenges in the practice of Healing Touch involves boundaries and dual relationships (e.g., patient versus friend). Perhaps the following "Touch Points" may prove helpful.

1. Safe Boundaries for the Masterful Practitioner

We practice loving kindness through establishing safe, professional boundaries. Boundaries clarify what will happen between the practitioner and patient. This means that sessions begin and end on time, confidentiality is maintained and records are kept safe, nothing is said outside of the session with the patient's consent, and our relationship with the patient is therapeutic, professional, and non-sexual.

Just by touching people, we have already crossed acceptable social norms. Our patients afford us more power in the session room than they would if they just saw us on the street. Simply by showing up, our patients are made vulnerable. Additionally, our patients experience non-ordinary or transpersonal states, and have unclear or absent boundaries through expanded states of consciousness. Thus, we must reinforce a safe environment by remaining centered, focused, and clear.

These safe boundaries keep the relationship focused upon the patient. People heal best when they have a safe environment. Boundaries keep us within the limits of our training (i.e., our scope of practice) and safe practice.

2. Do No Harm

As students, practitioners, and instructors of Healing Touch, our expertise comes from our professional training and our training in Healing Touch. We must know our professional limits and refer to appropriate experts. When in doubt or over our heads, we must place ourselves under supervision. In other words, we seek clarity and guidance from a mentor or counselor.

We do not flirt, date, or engage in romantic or sexual relationships with our patients. We take care of our own personal loneliness, isolation, and boredom elsewhere.

Even if a patient is determined to put us on a pedestal, we need to let them know that we are merely consultants who possess certain skills and training. At best, we know a small amount about a small area of the human condition. At highest action, we empower them to become a full partner in their healing journey.

3. Boundary Mistakes

Going beyond the boundaries of our expertise and our professional scope of practice is a common boundary mistake. Blurring the line between social and professional roles, ranging from chatting about ourselves during a session or turning a patient into a romantic partner, are also boundary mistakes.

Bending boundaries (e.g., "I don't usually do this, but this one time or in this case...") is a red flag or slippery slope. Beware the sense of rescue, such as feeling manipulated or trapped, feeling only you can help this patient, or being afraid if the patient does not get their own way.

4. Key Questions for Making Ethical Decisions

Does it align with the ethical principle of "Do No Harm"? Does it align with the ethical principle of "Do Good"? Does it align with the ethical principle of "Autonomy" (i.e., respecting a patient's self-authority and right to self-determination)? Does it maintain focus on the safety and well-being of the patient? Are you being respectful of the innate power imbalances within the therapeutic relationship? Does your behavior promote a dual relationship and make the therapeutic relationship less clear? Does your behavior stay within your scope of practice or does it exceed your area of expertise or the patient's consent? Does your action create a safe environment for the patient or diminish it? Could this action lead to less clarity or more challenge within the therapeutic relationship in the future?

5. Key Monitoring Points for the Practitioner

These points include the following: no sexual relationships with patients; examining prejudices and potentials for interference with the practitioner-patient relationship; monitoring financial entanglements and advantages; maintaining strict confidentiality and safeguarding records; falsifying or exaggerating outcome claims; and working within one's scope of practice.

6. Engage in Personal Growth Work

Obtain supervision with a peer or mentor. Consider using journaling as a means of self-reflection, or counseling for your own self-growth. Be kind to yourself and others, and seek help when you feel that you are getting in over your head. Receive Healing Touch from other colleagues and practitioners.

As we continue to evolve the profession of Healing Touch, each of us has the opportunity to bring forward a model of professionalism, high integrity, and holistic practice that truly supports the highest good of the client and, in turn, uplifts all of us who serve humanity through Healing Touch.

Legal Aspects of Biofield Therapy Practice

The legal basis for Healing Touch practice is the same as for manual and biofield interventions. The legal basis for practice is inherent under the auspices of the professional preparation of the practitioner who adds Healing Touch to his/her foundational discipline. The individual's professional discipline, educational preparation, and credentials provide the legal parameters for the practice of Healing Touch. This holds true for any manual and biofield therapy.

Healing Touch is a complementary therapy founded in nursing process. The continuing education in Healing Touch is designed to be incorporated within one's own educational and professional preparation. Within the United States, state regulatory laws have required both licensed health care professionals and lay individuals to practice within their scope of practice and training.

A number of states within the United States have passed Health Freedom Laws to allow unlicensed health care providers to advertise and provide their services legally, while complying with certain requirements specific within the law. As of March 2017, ten states have enacted health freedom laws, including Idaho, Oklahoma, Minnesota, California, Rhode Island, Louisiana, Arizona, New Mexico, Colorado, and Nevada. More states continue to be added.

Essentially, these health care laws allow the public to have access to unlicensed complementary care practitioners provided they comply with certain conditions. Most of these laws require that unlicensed practitioners must disclose to patients their credentials, that they are not a licensed physician or health care provider, their service or therapy is not licensed by the state and is alternative or complementary to licensed healing arts services, and a description of their service and the rationale behind it. A description of Healing Touch can be found in Chapter One.

These laws prohibit the unlicensed practitioners from invasive or diagnostic procedures. These laws include, but are not limited to, performing surgery, setting fractures, administering x-ray radiation, prescribing drugs or controlled substances, directly manipulating the joints or spine, physically invading the body except for topical non-harmful and non-prescription applications, recommending discontinuation of current medical treatment prescribed by a licensed health care practitioner, making a specific medical diagnosis, or engaging in unethical behavior or behavior that would be otherwise prohibited under state law.

The National Health Freedom Coalition is an organization with the mission of:

> Promoting access to all health care information, services, treatments and products that the people deem beneficial for their own health and survival; to promote an understanding of the laws and factors impacting the right to access; and to promote the health of the people of this nation [the United States].

It is important for you to become very familiar with the regulatory laws in your state or provence, and if a lay practitioner, consider becoming involved in a Health Freedom Law movement within your area.

Practicum and Certification

Training in and certification as a practitioner of Healing Touch follows a mentorship model and portfolio process. This model is grounded in traditional mentorship models throughout the ages for artisans and healers, as well as contemporary training in conventional health care including nursing and other allied health professionals. The mentorship aligns with a practicum process in which individuals move from novice to accomplished through practice of the therapy, case management, educational activities, expansion of self care and knowledge of integrative health, reflection, and community service. Summation of these activities make up the portfolio to be reviewed for certification. This portfolio process has long been used in health care professions, as well as artistic and creative endeavors, to demonstrate the breadth and depth of one's work in a field of study or area of expertise. The portfolio represents more than merely an examination; rather the portfolio represents a well-rounded practitioner of healing arts.

The practicum experience begins upon the successful completion of the Healing Touch course titled Case Management and Professional Practice. Following this course, students of Healing Touch identify a mentor to guide their practicum experience as they refine their case management and Healing Touch practice skills while engaging in educational activities and personal growth work. The mentor, who is a Certified Healing Touch Practitioner, works in tandem with the student to develop a mentorship plan and contract that the practicum will follow. Regular interaction between the mentor and student is essential, as is open communication, trust, mutual respect, and an intention for the highest good and success of the student. Mentors should strive to provide enthusiasm for the student and their work, sensitivity to the personal journey of the practicum experience, appreciation for individual differences, respect for self and the student, unselfishness, support, and clear communication (Lee, Dennis, & Campbell, 2007). In addition to case management, which is discussed in more detail later in this chapter, the practicum experience involves educational and personal growth activities.

A professional profile consisting of a notebook and resume are developed during the practicum process as a reflection of one's professional practice, education and training, skills and expertise, and personal growth as a practitioner and healer.

Practitioners and healers must have knowledge and familiarity with healing practices and traditions. This is accomplished during the practicum through a self-directed reading and education program, as well as experiential learning and self care through engaging in other healing modalities. Educational experiences through reading, lectures, conferences, and workshops broaden the understanding in healing through a focus on Healing Touch, energy medicine and holism, quantum physics, spiritual development, personal and professional development, ethics, and journaling. Additionally, experiencing a number of other complementary and integrative healing modalities and therapies increases one's knowledge of healing traditions, fosters a professional network of healers for referrals, and supports self care and personal growth.

Community engagement through service and networking are keys to successful development as a practitioner. These activities during the practicum period afford students the opportunity to share Healing Touch with their wider community as an act service, allowing students to live out the Attributes of the Heart as described by Joy from Chapter Two.

Specific guidelines of the requirements for the practicum, as well as the certification portfolio, can be found on the Healing Beyond Borders website and will be discussed in the Case Management and Professional Practice and Self-Evaluation and Professional Development courses.

Case Management

A significant portion of the practicum process is refinement of case management skills by the student. Case management refers to the ability to work with patients over time using the framework described in Chapter Four. Case management might involve working with someone over a series of several sessions, or a single session, and involves using the session framework guideline to provide holistic, person-centered care to the patient. During the practicum experience, healing sessions are fully documented sessions as work toward completing the final course in the Healing Touch training series, Self-Evaluation and Professional Development. Documentation follows the guidelines discussed in Chapter Four.

From these documented sessions, case studies will be drawn as part of the portfolio. A single case study summarizing the case management of one patient over time is written in depth following the guidelines provided in the certification portfolio application. This case study is a full description of the case management process and healing session framework, demonstrating the student's ability to provide appropriate, meaningful care. In addition to this full case study, two brief case studies highlighting the use of specific Healing Touch techniques are prepared to demonstrate proficiency in the use and application of these techniques.

References

Anselme, L. (2014). Ethical underpinnings: Respecting and honoring the soul. In D. Wardell, S. Kagel, and L. Anselme (Eds.), *Healing Touch: Enhancing life through energy therapy* (pp. 159-185). Bloomington, IN: iUniverse.

Anselme, L. (2003-2007) The Ethics of Touch Series, Part 1-8, *Healing Touch International Newsletter*, Lakewood, CO: Healing Touch International, Inc.

Benjamin, B., & Sohnen-Moe, C. (2003). *The ethics of touch*. Tucson, AZ: SMA, Inc.

Dalai Lama. (1999). *Ethics for the new millennium*. New York, NY: Penguin Putnam.

Healing Touch International, Inc. (1996) International Code of Ethics / Standards of Practice for healing touch practitioners and students. Lakewood, CO: Healing Beyond Borders.

Healing Touch International, Inc. (2000) Scope of Practice Statement. Lakewood, CO: Healing Beyond Borders.

(Lee, A., Dennis, C., & Campbell, P. (2007). Nature's guide for mentors. *Nature*, 447, 791-797.

National Health Freedom Coalition. http://www.nationalhealthfreedom.org.

Tylor, K. (1995). *The ethics of caring: Honoring the web of life in our professional healing relationships*. Santa Cruz, CA: Hanford Mead Publishing.

Appendix

HEALING TOUCH INTERNATIONAL
HEALING TOUCH CERTIFICATE PROGRAM
COURSE LISTINGS AND DESCRIPTIONS

FOUNDATIONS OF HEALING TOUCH

Course Description:

The theoretical concepts which underlie holistic healthcare practices are explored along with how they relate to the core values which guide the practice of Healing Touch. Healing Touch techniques used in the etheric field are acquired along with an understanding of how they interface with the human biofield.

ENERGETIC PATTERNING AND CLINICAL APPLICATIONS
Pre-requisite, completion of Foundations of Healing Touch

Course Description:

The skill of completing an intake interview that identifies patterns of behaviors for which Healing Touch techniques may be useful in assisting a patient to re-pattern their energy field is acquired. Healing Touch techniques learned in the foundation course are integrated into applications that assist in re-patterning spinal health. The appreciation of Healing Touch progresses to a deeper level with the acquisition of a technique to assist the patient in expanding their heart energy.

ADVANCED HEALER PREPARATION
Pre-requisite, completion of Energetic Patterning and Clinical Applications

Course Description:

Methods of raising one's energetic vibration are acquired that facilitate the student's application of techniques that can be utilized with upper energetic field layers.

CASE MANAGEMENT AND PROFESSIONAL PRACTICE
Pre-requisite, completion of Advanced Healer Preparation

Course Description:

To align with the responsibilities of professional practice, this course is a practicum in which case management is implemented and multiple Healing Touch sessions are delivered over a period of time.

SELF-EVALUATION AND PROFESSIONAL DEVELOPMENT
Pre-requisite, completion of Case Management and Professional Practice

Course Description:

Completed mentorship activities are reviewed and evaluated to assist the students in identifying activities that can help them to grow in their professional practitioner role.

Notice of Privacy Practices for Healing Touch Clients

This notice describes how health information about you may be used and disclosed and how you can get access to this information. Please carefully review this notice.

As a provider of Healing Touch, I am committed to protecting health information about you. I create a record of our interactions and the services that you receive from me for use in your health care and Healing Touch treatment. Typically, this record contains information regarding your health history, symptoms you may be experiencing, physical health and energy assessment, nursing diagnosis, intervention, and proposed plan of care. This health information will only be utilized to the extent necessary to provide you with quality health care.

My Responsibility. I am required by law to:
- Ensure that health information that identifies you is kept private and confidential.
- Give you this Notice of my legal duties and privacy practices with respect to your health information.
- Follow the terms of this Notice as long as it is in effect. If I revise this notice, I will follow the terms of the revised Notice as long as the revised Notice is in effect.

I. **How I may use or disclose your health information**

   Treatment / Intervention: The type and amounts of your health information provided to other health care providers within our practice will be limited to relevant and appropriate information needed to provide you care and treatment.

   Payment: I may disclose your health information to third party payers, such as your insurance company, Medicare or Medicaid or worker's compensation in order to receive payment or support your reimbursement for services rendered.

   Regular Health Care Operations: I may be required to disclose your health information in order to review my services for purposes of quality assurance, inspection or audit. I may disclose health information to other health care providers to the extent necessary for them to provide you the appropriate level of care and treatment. To the extent allowed by law, I may release Health Information about you to a family member, other relative, or close personal friend who is involved in your health care if the health information released is directly relevant to such person's involvement with your care.

   To avert a serious threat to health and safety: I may use and disclose health information about you when necessary to prevent a serious threat to your health and safety or to the health and safety of another person or the general public. Any disclosure, however, would only be to someone who is able to help prevent the threat.

   Research: I may disclose your health information to researchers conducting research that has been approved by an institutional review board and for which you have given informed consent.

- **Judicial:** administrative proceedings or law enforcement activities: I may disclose your health information in the course of any administrative or judicial proceeding, during lawsuits and disputes and for certain law enforcement activities.
- **Public Health:** I may disclose your health information to public health authorities for purposes related to: preventing or controlling disease, injury or disability; reporting child or adult abuse or neglect; reporting domestic violence; reporting disease or infection exposure.
- **Appointment Reminders:** I may use and disclose health information in order to contact you as a reminder that you have an appointment with me.
- **Special Privacy Protections for Alcohol and Drug Abuse Information:** Alcohol and drug abuse health information has special privacy protections. I will not disclose any information identifying a client as being a patient, or provide any health information relating to a client's substance abuse treatment unless: (a) the client consents in writing; (b) a court order requires disclosure of the information; (c) health personnel need the information to meet a health emergency; (d) it is necessary to report a crime or a threat to commit a crime, or to report abuse or neglect as required by law.

II. When I may not use or disclose your health information

Except as described in this Notice of Privacy Practices, I will not use or disclose your health information without your written authorization. If you do authorize me to use or disclose your health information for another purpose, you may revoke your authorization in writing at any time. A revocation of authorization will be effective on the date it is received and will not affect previous disclosures.

III. Your Health Information Rights

- **Right to request restriction.** You may request restrictions on certain uses and disclosure of your health information. I am not required to agree to that restriction that you request.
- **Right to confidential communications.** You may request that I communicate confidential information in a certain way or at a certain location, but you must specify how or where you wish to be contacted.
- **Right to inspect and copy.** You have the right to inspect and copy your health information; however, I may decline to release certain psychotherapy records if in my opinion the release may be harmful to your health. You may be charged a nominal fee for requested copies of your health information record.
- **Right to request amendment.** You have a right to request that I amend your health information that is incorrect or incomplete. I am not required to change your health information and will inform you if your request is denied and how you can disagree with the denial.
- **Right to accounting of disclosures.** You have a right to request a list of the disclosures of your health information that have

been made to persons or institutions other than for health care treatment, payment or operations in the past six years.

Right to a copy of this notice. You may request a paper copy of this Notice of Privacy Practices.

IV. Changes to Notice of Privacy Practices

I reserve the right to amend this Notice of Privacy Practices at any time in the future, and to make the new provisions effective for all information that it maintains, including information that was created or received prior to the date of such change. Until such an amendment is made, I am required by law to comply with this notice. In the event that changes are made to this Notice, you will be provided with a written copy at your next treatment session with me. You may also request a copy of the Privacy Policy at any time.

I have read the above statement and have been informed of my rights:

Signed: _____ Date: _____

© Health Care Integration Booklet, Healing Touch International, Inc. 2000. All Rights Reserved

Healing Beyond Borders
Educating and Certifying the Healing Touch ®

Health Care Facility Policy and Procedure

Definition Healing Touch
Healing Touch is a National Institutes of Health classified biofield therapy and nursing intervention that contains a group of standardized, noninvasive techniques that clear, energize, and balance the human and environmental energy fields. Gentle touch assists in balancing physical, mental, emotional and spiritual well-being. It is safe for all ages and works in harmony with standard medical care. Healing Touch may be used to address the NANDA-1 nursing diagnosis of "Imbalanced Energy Field" that identifies a disruption in the flow of energy surrounding a person that results in a disharmony of the body, mind, and/or spirit.

Policy
Healing Touch complements and is adjunctive to therapeutic interventions utilized by physicians and other licensed health care providers. Healing Touch is an independent nursing intervention utilizing nursing process and does not require a physician order nor does it require formal informed consent. However, the nurse must have permission to assist the client. In addition, nurses who use Healing Touch as an intervention must have successfully completed at the minimum, an eighteen hour continuing education Foundations in Healing Touch course taught by a Certified Healing Touch Instructor. Within the acute care setting, it is highly recommended that the nurse will have successfully completed the next sequential course of Energetic Patterns and Clinical Applications.

There are five courses within the HTI Healing Touch Certificate Program curriculum that leads to completion of the course of study. Healing Beyond Borders defines several levels of Healing Touch practice: the Student, a Practitioner who has completed the 105 contact hour program of study and has received a Certificate of Completion by Healing Beyond Borders, and a Certified Healing Touch Practitioner, who has met certification criteria and competency and has been approved by the Healing Beyond Borders Certification Board.

Indications for use include but are not limited to:
Pain, acute and chronic Fear and Anxiety
Promotion of health and well being Spiritual distress
Impaired tissue integrity Respiratory distress
Post utilization of anesthesia, chemotherapy and other toxins

The following are approved Healing Touch interventions:
Celestial and Ketheric Repatterning, Chakra Connection, Chakra Energizing, Chakra Spread, Chelation, Deep Auric Clearing, Etheric Template Repatterning, Field Repatterning, Glymphatic System Support, Hopi Technique, Laser, Modified Mesmeric Clearing, Noel's Mind Clearing, Scudder Meridian Clearing, Siphon, Spinal Clearing and Energizing, Spinal Flush, Spiral Meditation, Pain Management (Pain Ridge, Pain Spike, Energetic Suture and Wound Closure), Headache Management

Appendix

References

Anderson, J. G., & Taylor, A. G. (2011). Effects of Healing Touch in clinical practice: A systematic review of randomized clinical trials. *Journal of Holistic Nursing* 29, 221-228.

Anderson, J.G., Anselme, L.A., Hart, L.K. (2017). Foundations and Practice of Healing Touch. Lakewood, CO: Healing Beyond Borders.

Anselme, L. (2007). HTI Healing Touch and Health Care Integration, 7th Ed., Lakewood, CO: Lakewood, CO.

Barrett, E. A. M. (1990). *Visions of Rogers' science-based nursing*. New York NY: National League for Nursing.

Bradford, M.(1993). *The Healing Energy of Your Hands*. Berkeley, CA: Crossing Press.

Brennan, B. (1987). *Hands of Light: A guide to healing through the human energy field*. NY: Bantam Books.

Brennan, B. (1993). *Light Emerging: The journey of personal health*. NY: Bantam Books.

Bruyere, R. (1989) *Wheels of Light: A Study of the Chakras*. Arcadia, CA: Bon Productions.

Durkheim, K. (1975). *Hara: The Vital Center of Man*. Sandpoint, ID: Morning Light Press.

Eschiti, V. S. (2007). Healing touch: A low-tech intervention in high-tech settings. *Dimensions of Critical Care Nursing* 26, 9-14.

Jain, S., & Mills, P. J. (2010). Biofield therapies: Helpful or full of hype? A best evidence synthesis. *International Journal of Behavioral Medicine* 17, 1-16.

Joy, W. B. (1979). *Joy's way: A map for the transformational journey*. New York, NY: Jeremy P. Tarcher/Putnam.

King, R. P. (2005). The integration of healing touch with conventional care at the Scripps Center for Integrative Medicine. *Explore* 1, 144-145.

Markides, K.C. (1987) *Homage to the sun: The wisdom of the magus of Strovolos*. London: Penguin Group Ltd. Arkana.

Noel, R. (2011). *The Huggin' Healer*. Baltimore, MD: Publish America.

North American Nursing Diagnosis Association. (2014) NANDA Nursing Diagnosis: Definitions & Classification. Philadelphia, PA: Wiley Blackwell.

Oschman, J. (2000). *Energy medicine: The scientific basis*. New York, NY: Churchill Livingstone.

So, P. S., Jiang, Y., & Qin, Y. (2008). Touch therapies for pain relief in adults. *Cochrane Database of Systematic Reviews*, Issue 4.

Wardell, D., Kagel, S., & Anselme, L. (2014). *Healing Touch: Enhancing life through energy therapy*. Bloomington, IN: iUniverse.

Resources

Healing Beyond Borders
445 Union Blvd. Suite
Lakewood, CO 80228 (303) 989 – 7982 Fax (303) 980-8683
Email: education@healingbeyondborders.org
www.HealingBeyondBorders.org

Created: 4/1998, Revised: 9/03, 8/07, 9/09, 7/10, 2/14, 4/15, 4/17
© Healing Touch International, Inc.

Healing Beyond Borders
Educating and Certifying the Healing Touch ®

Sample Healing Touch Informed Consent
Practitioner Name/Credentials
or
Facility or Service Program/Department Name

My Healing Touch Practitioner has discussed the following with me and I understand that:

- Healing Touch is light, gentle touch on or near the body. I will be fully clothed or draped appropriately and will lie comfortably upon a massage table or recline in a chair. Gentle touch assists in balancing my physical, mental, emotional and spiritual well-being, supporting my natural ability to self-heal.
- Research suggests that there are many possible benefits in receiving Healing Touch, including reducing stress, calming anxiety, decreasing pain, creating a sense of well-being, strengthening the immune system, enhancing recovery from surgery, deepening a spiritual connection, and more. Individual experiences will vary.
- Healing Touch supports standard medical care and is not intended to replace appropriate medical intervention or therapy.
- My Healing Touch Practitioner recommends that I be under the care of a qualified medical provider for any health problems and that I inform them that I am receiving Healing Touch.
- My Healing Touch Practitioner will operate within their scope of practice. (This varies according to their health care licensure: e.g. Registered Nurse, Counselor, Massage Therapist, Medical Doctor, etc.).
- My Healing Touch Practitioner will conduct his/her practice according to accepted standards and ethics as approved by Healing Beyond Borders.
- My Healing Touch Practitioner has made no specific claims regarding results that I may receive from Healing Touch sessions.
- I understand that I am encouraged to provide feedback at any time to my Healing Touch Practitioner regarding my comfort in order to adjust or complete the session.
- I have been given an opportunity to clarify any questions I may have about Healing Touch.

I give my consent to receive Healing Touch.

_____   _____
Printed Name   Date

_____
Signature

© Healing Touch International, Inc. 2000 Used with Permission

Appendix 121

Initial Assessment for a Healing Touch Session

Initials _____ Gender Identity _____ DOB ___/___/___

Phone _____ Email _____

Address _____

Date ___/___/___ Session # _____

Physical Presentation

   Mobility
   Mood
   Comfort

Reason for Session

   Signs & Symptoms of Complaint
   Aggravating Factors
   Current Interventions

Personal Information

   Family Structure
   Living arrangement
   Employment
   Social Life
      Spiritual affiliation
      Other important organizations
      Major Stress factors
   Self Care
      Nutrition
      Sleep pattern
      Exercise
      Spiritual Practices

Medical History

      Current problems & interventions used

      Chronic problems & care providers

Surgeries

Injuries

Family illnesses history

Medication / Supplements

Energetic Assessments

Chakras
Field Shape & Size
Areas of Congestion

Problems: (Prioritize)

Mutual Goals
Short Term

Long Term

Intervention(s) & Energy Shifts Noted

Evaluation, Referrals, Recommendations

Appendix   123

Follow-up Healing Touch Session

Initials _____ Session # _____ Date ___/___/_____

Interval History

Energetic Assessments
- Chakras
- Field Shape & Size
- Areas of Congestion

Problems: (Prioritize)

Updated Mutual Goals
- Short Term

- Long Term

Intervention(s) & Energy Shifts Noted

Evaluation, Referrals, Recommendations